GECON 2006

GECON 2006

Proceedings of the 3rd International Workshop on Grid Economics and Business Models

Singapore 16 May 2006

Editors

Hing-Yan Lee
National Grid Office, Singapore

Steven Miller
Singapore Management University, Singapore

National Grid
NG
SINGAPORE

SMU
SINGAPORE MANAGEMENT UNIVERSITY

World Scientific

NEW JERSEY • LONDON • SINGAPORE • BEIJING • SHANGHAI • HONG KONG • TAIPEI • CHENNAI

Published by

World Scientific Publishing Co. Pte. Ltd.
5 Toh Tuck Link, Singapore 596224
USA office: 27 Warren Street, Suite 401-402, Hackensack, NJ 07601
UK office: 57 Shelton Street, Covent Garden, London WC2H 9HE

British Library Cataloguing-in-Publication Data
A catalogue record for this book is available from the British Library.

GECON 2006
Proceedings of the 3rd International Workshop on Grid Economics and Business Models

ISBN 981-256-821-2

Printed in Singapore by World Scientific Printers (S) Pte Ltd

Welcome Message

I warmly welcome you to the 3rd International Workshop on Grid Economics and Business Models held for the first time in Singapore.

Hosting this workshop is timely, especially as the Phase 2 of National Grid is presently focusing its efforts on raising awareness and promoting the adoption of Grid Computing by business and industry users in Singapore.

While setting up and operating enterprise grids are well understood and there have been many successful deployments, we need to undertake much more work to understand the issues pertaining to the Grid economy. Such issues include software licensing, pricing of Grid services and resource usage, accounting, legal and taxation matters, and business strategies.

We have, in the past year, conducted trials and proof-of-concepts on Grid deployment for business and industry users in Singapore. In these pilot projects, we have worked with users from the R&D, digital media and manufacturing communities. Our experience reveals that for narrow domains, there exist specific solutions though these are not scalable in general. It is through real deployment that we will be able to glean insight and understanding on the dynamics underlying the Grid economy. Even then, experiences in different countries may differ, as the target beneficiaries may be huge corporations in one while they may be small and medium- sized enterprises in another. What is clear is there remains much to be done in terms of experimentation, early deployment, and sharing of lessons.

Finally, I wish you all a productive and successful workshop. I sincerely hope that your deliberations will throw some light on the outstanding issues and move the operational and deployment of Grid economy forward.

Thank you.

Rear-Admiral (Retired) Richard Lim
Chairman, National Grid Steering Committee
Singapore
May 2006

Preface

The 3rd International Workshop on Grid Economics and Business Models (GECON 2006) is being held in Singapore, in conjunction with the IEEE Cluster Computing & Grid Conference (CCGrid 2006) and GridAsia 2006. The CCGrid and GridAsia events provide ample evidence that worldwide efforts to design, build and apply distributed computing systems based on Grid paradigms, design principles and technology tools are rapidly increasing. There are a growing number of examples to demonstrate the feasibility and potential power of this approach.

We have all witnessed how a large fraction of the world's population has been impacted by infocomms-enabled connectivity over the past two decades. The effects are felt on a personal and professional level as well as on the societal level. Three of the technology waves that have driven this connectivity are:

1. the growth of wireless phone and device usage;
2. the increase in fixed and mobile internet access; and
3. the explosion in worldwide web usage.

In addition, there are the vast numbers of applications and services, supported by or derived from these three foundations of modern global connectivity.

Participants in the Grid Computing community feel they are on the verge of setting in motion yet another important wave. This latest Grid wave leverages the connectivity infrastructure and capabilities of the preceding waves noted above. Now increasingly sophisticated virtual collaborations, requiring larger and larger amounts of computer and storage resources, can be more easily and economically achieved through virtually connecting, loosely-coupled IT resources distributed across a diverse set of participants.

There is a sense that something new, really important, and perhaps even paradigm changing could result from the developments occurring in the world of Grid Computing. At the same time it is hard to deny a *déjà vu* sense that, "we have all been here before" or that trends are coming around full circle. After all, in the mid-1940s the modern era of digital computing started with the practice of 'shared services'. When there were only a small number of mainframes, nearly all IT users obtained computing and storage services from centralized resource owners (either the captive or commercial IT service bureau provider) on an as-needed basis, often on a pay-per-use basis.

So, if there is an emerging Grid wave (whatever its size), will the associated economic and business model issues be any different from what was experienced decades ago?

We know the story of how IT has evolved over the past fifty plus years. There have been decades of improvements in computing and software technology. And there were several paradigm changing hardware/software waves: e.g. mini computers, personal computers, client-server, networked computing and the web. These technological and application advancements have driven parallel developments in the related commercial and business areas. And they have impacted higher-level economic and policy issues affecting industries, sectors and society as a whole.

This raises an interesting issue. Based on over fifty years of commercial experience with IT, shouldn't we already know most everything one would need to know about any conceivable economic, policy or business model issue relating to Grid Computing?

Industry practitioners and university researchers interested in the impacts of IT from an economics perspective have been looking at the key economic issues – the nature of competition, incentive and market mechanisms, pricing strategies, profit generation, and the balancing of supply and demand at the level of industries, sectors and economies.

Similarly, in the last few decades, managers and firms providing any type of IT or communications driven service have had to work out their own business models to make decisions about such business basics as:

1. targeting which services to sell and how those services will be bundled
2. who the customers will be
3. the 'value-proposition' that provides the compelling story for why the customer should pay for the services provided
4. how to charge for the services in order to stay in business and eventually obtain the greatest possible revenue

Management science researchers have looked at these issues as well, and contributed a number of models and methods to aid this type of decision making.

Let's come back to the question of, "Shouldn't we already know how to handle the economic and business model issues related to Grid Computing?" If not based on our cumulative experience of past decades, then perhaps based on our most recent experiences in the last few years. Or, perhaps the emerging reality is that Grid Computing itself, or Grid in convergence with other evolving technological, business and economic forces, is creating situations and scenarios that are substantially different than what has been seen before. And as a result, the community of people pushing the Grid wave forward, as well as those trying to ride the wave (through buying or otherwise leveraging these services) don't really know how to adopt and modify previous economic and business model knowledge to fit the new situation.

Or maybe we do know how to address these economic and business model issues. But maybe there are a few new wrinkles, such as concerns for privacy of information in shared distributed systems, or challenges with licensing commercial software applications across multiple nodes and resource owners of a public grid. And while these types of 'soft issues' are not entirely without precedent, the centrality and complexity of these types of problems in the Grid Computing setting amplifies these issues to a new scale and level of difficulty. This could mean that the propagation of the Grid wave is being held back by vexing and complicated 'soft issues' related to individual and marketplace incentives, governance and policy.

The purpose of this workshop is to bring together a community of people who can help answer these questions. Workshop presenters include a group of distinguished management scientists and applied economists who understand the existing body and emerging frontiers of theory and university-based research pertaining to the economics of IT. Workshop presenters also come from some of the world's most active industrial R&D labs. These presenters are working on developing Grid technologies *and* on identifying and addressing economic and business model issues dealing with Grid-related resource allocation and management. Other presenters hail from companies and countries experimenting with medium and large-scale application and deployed projects. They are experimenting with putting all of the pieces together for Grid-based service delivery, the technology pieces as well as the management, governance, economic, and policy pieces.

The workshop participants can help us understand the extent to which insights and models from current and historical experience with IT commercialization can be applied to the emerging Grid-computing scenarios. They can tell us whether and how Grid, or Grid in convergence with other existing and emerging forces, is creating situations that are qualitatively different from what has been experienced previously. If this is the case (to whatever degree), our participants can give guidance on how we can best adapt our existing body of economic and business model experience to deal with this novelty. And if there are a 'critical few' knotty and elusive problems in the realm of governance, policy or incentives that are neither purely technological or economic or business model in nature, but seem to be at the root of what is holding back the propagation of the Grid wave, then our workshop participants need to show us how to understand and address these issues.

In essence, this workshop is designed to be a human-powered Grid, where we can connect with one another, pool our intellectual resources, and make progress on large, complex problems faster than any of us could do individually.

We owe a debt of gratitude to the hard-work and contributions made by the program and organizing committees towards making this workshop a success. We hope that these proceedings will serve a useful reference on the Grid economics and business models.

Finally, do have a great time in Singapore!

STEVEN MILLER
School of Information Systems
Singapore Management University

LEE HING YAN
National Grid Office, Singapore

Workshop Committees

Workshop Co-Chairs

Hing-Yan Lee (National Grid Office, Singapore)
Steven Miller (Singapore Management University)

Organizing Committee

Choo Thong Tiong (National Grid Office, Singapore)
Jon Lau Khee-Erng (National Grid Office, Singapore)
Danny Oh Chin Hock (Singapore Management University)
Tan Puay Siang (Singapore Management University)
Nigel Teow (National Grid Office, Singapore)
Vasugi d/o Vellusamy (National Grid Office, Singapore)

Program Committee

Jorn Altmann (International University in Germany)
Hermant K. Bhargava (UC Davis, USA)
Rajkumar Buyya (University of Melbourne, Australia)
John Chuang (UC Berkeley, USA)
John Darlington (Imperial College, UK)
Kartik Hosenager (University of Pennsylvania, USA)
Junseok Hwang (Seoul National University, Korea)
Ramayya Krishnan (Carnegie Mellon University, USA)
Kevin Lai (HP Labs, USA)
Jysoo Lee (KISTI, Korea)
Dirk Neumann (Karlsruhe University, Germany)
David Parkes (Harvard University, USA)
Simon See (Sun Microsystems, Singapore)
Satoshi Sekiguchi (AIST, Japan)
Yoshio Tanaka (AIST, Japan)
Maria Tsakali (European Commission, Belgium)

Contents

Grid Economy Test-beds & Operation

EVALUATING DEMAND PREDICTION TECHNIQUES FOR COMPUTATIONAL MARKETS

THOMAS SANDHOLM

KTH – Royal Institute of Technolog,
SE-100 44 Stockholm, Sweden,
E-mail: sandholm@pdc.kth.se

KEVIN LAI

Informations Dynamics Laboratory,
HP Labs, Palo Alto, CA 94304
E-mail: kevin.lai@hp.com

We evaluate different prediction techniques to estimate future demand of resource usage in a computational market. Usage traces from the PlanetLab network are used to compare the prediction accuracy of models based on histograms, normal distribution approximation, maximum entropy, and autoregression theory. We particularly study the ability to predict the tail of the probability distribution in order to give guarantees of upper bounds of demand. We found that the maximum entropy model was particularly well suited to predict these upper bounds.

1. Introduction

Large scale shared computational Grids allow more efficient usage of resources through statistical multiplexing. Economic allocation of resources in such systems provide a variety of benefits including allocating resources to users who benefit from them the most, encouraging organizations to share resources, and providing accountability [12,6,1,14].

One critical issue for economic allocation systems is predictability. Users require the ability to predict future prices for resources so that they can plan their budgets. Without predictability, users will either over-spend, sacrificing future performance, or over-save, sacrificing current performance. Both lead to dissatisfaction and instability. Moreover, the lack of accurate information precludes rational behavior, which would disrupt the operation of the many allocation mechanisms that depend on rational behavior.

There are three parts to predictability: the predictability provided by the allocation mechanism, the predictability of the users' behavior, and the predictability provided by statistical algorithms used to model the behavior. We examine the latter two. Consequently, these results are not dependent on a specific allocation mechanism and instead apply to many systems.

The goal of this paper is to examine the degree to which future demand can be predicted from previous demand in a shared computing platform. Ideally, we would use the pricing data from a heavily used economic grid system, but such systems have not yet been widely deployed. Instead, we examine PlanetLab[9], a widely-distributed, shared computing platform with a highly flexible and fluid allocation mechanism. The PlanetLab data set has the advantage of encompassing many users and hosts and having very little friction for allocation. However, PlanetLab does not use economic allocation, so we substitute usage as a proxy for pricing. Since many economic allocation mechanisms (e.g., Spawn[11], Popcorn[10], ICE[4], and Tycoon[7]) adjust prices in response to the demand, we believe that this approximation is appropriate.

We examine this data set using four different statistical prediction algorithms: histogram (Hist) approximation, maximum entropy (MaxEnt) density estimation, an autoregression (AR) time series model, and a normal (Norm) distribution model. We evaluated these algorithms by feeding them samples of usage data over a particular period of time and then measuring the error of the generated model. We then measured the error of using these models to predict future demand.

Our findings are as follows:

• MaxEnt and Norm were able to accurately model the data set over larger time periods. Maximum entropy estimation is approximately twice as accurate as a normal model because of its ability to capture skewness. Both methods are an order of magnitude more accurate than histogram approximation. The MaxEnt model is based on fitting integrals of the distribution function to statistical moments. This fit may not yield satisfactory approximations if the number of data samples in the time window investigated are too few, and we then fall back to the normal distribution approximation.

• All of the techniques produce inaccurate predictions, when trying to predict the cumulative distribution function for future demand. Autoregression has the additional disadvantage of requiring so much compute overhead that it was not able to complete some predictions. Furthermore, the AR model requires more history data to be maintained in order to retrain the prediction model to fit the current load.

• Despite inaccurate predictions of the full cumulative distribution function, MaxEnt and Norm were able to produce accurate *bounds* for demand. This is important because bounds are sufficient for users to budget. For example, if a user knows that the probability of hosts being less than $1 per host within the next week is 99%, and he needs 10 hosts, then he knows he should budget $10.

2. Prediction Algorithms

The goal of the prediction algorithms is to predict the demand for a resource based on historical data. In an economic system, the demand determines the price, which allows users to budget accurately. The general prediction model we use is summarized here.

$$P(Y \leq \frac{y-\mu}{\sigma}) = \Phi(\frac{y-\mu}{\sigma}) \tag{1}$$

$$y \leq \mu + \sigma\Phi^{-1}(p) \tag{2}$$

where y is the demand with mean μ and standard deviation σ, and Φ is the cumulative probability density function (CDF) of a normal distribution. Eq. 1 gives us a way to get a probability of a demand given its mean and standard deviation, and Eq. 2 allows us to find the demand corresponding to level of guarantee or probability.

In this work we want to remove the assumption of a normal distribution, and instead only assume an iid (independent identically distributed) distribution, and then compare the results to those obtained using the normal distribution assumption. More specifically, this means that we want to take the skewness of the distribution into consideration in our predictions. This extension is motivated by previous work on computational markets and usage behavior on the web [3] have shown that heavy-tailed distributions are common.

We evaluate three different approaches to tackle this generalization here, histogram (Hist) approximation, maximum entropy (MaxEnt) density estimation, and an autoregression (AR) time series model. The results are benchmarked against approximations used with the normal (Norm) distribution assumption, and compared to the real outcome.

The Hist approximation is based on placing sample data points in a fixed number of bins with predetermined data ranges. It therefore assumes some a-priori knowledge of the variance of the data. In our benchmarks we used 10 and 100 bins to approximate the distribution of values in a range of about 5000 distinct data values.

The MaxEnt model is based on the concept of choosing a distribution function which maximizes the entropy or randomness (or simply the unknown parameters) of a function given some characteristics such as statistical moments. This idea was first articulated by E.T. Jaynes in [5]. Cover and Thomas [2] then proved that all functions maximizing the entropy of a distribution are of a general form. For example, given the following constraints of the three moments about the origin μ_1, μ_2, μ_3

$$\int_{-\infty}^{\infty} f(x)dx = 1, \int_{-\infty}^{\infty} xf(x)dx = \mu_1, \int_{-\infty}^{\infty} x^2 f(x)dx = \mu_2, \int_{-\infty}^{\infty} x^3 f(x)dx = \mu_3$$

then the distribution function that maximizes the entropy has the form

$$f(x) = e^{\lambda_0 + \lambda_1 x + \lambda_2 x^2 + \lambda_3 x^3}$$

Now the problem of finding the distribution function f reduces to finding the λ parameters. Cover and Thomas suggests starting with the parameters known for a normal distribution and then "wiggle" them to find the best fit. In our implementation we performed this "wiggling" by applying the steepest descent iterative optimization algorithm described in [13]. In summary, we iteratively try to get closer to

$$\theta = \lambda_0, \lambda_1, \lambda_2, \lambda_3$$

by initializing it to the values know for a normal distribution and then assigning it subsequent values according to

$$\theta_{t+1} = \theta_t - \mathrm{H}^{-1}\mathrm{B}$$

where H is the Hessian matrix defined as

$$H_{k,j} = \int x^k x^j f(x, \theta_t)dx, 0 \leq k, j \leq 3$$

and B is the difference vector

$$B_k = \int x^k f(x, \theta_t)dx - \mu_k, 0 \leq k \leq 3$$

Note that we use the first three moments to capture the skewness of the distribution. Using more than three moments introduces irregular fluctuations which could prevent the algorithm from converging, and it also more easily runs into numerical limitations such us number overflows and round off errors.

The AR model [8] is a standard time-series model of the following form

$$X_t = \mu + \sum_{i=1}^{k} \alpha_i (X_{t-1} - \mu)$$

where μ is the measured mean in the training data, and k is the order (we used $k = 2$ in our benchmarks). The model parameters α_i are estimated by first calculating the autocorrelation vector for the training data and then solving the Yule-Walker equations. Note that the white-noise parameter has been omitted for simplicity.

Four different evaluations are performed on time series data using these techniques. First, we look at how well the summary data, such as bin density with Hist, the first three moments about the origin with MaxEnt, and the first two moments with Norm approximate the distribution described in the current period. If we have an iid distribution this should also give an indication of the possible accuracy of future predictions. Second, we look at how well predictions based on approximations of the cumulative density function in previous intervals can predict future distributions, and compare that to AR prediction results. Third, we look at how the actual distribution changes over time in the different intervals studied. Finally we look at how well the 99th percentile of the cumulative distribution function can be estimated in order to see how well guarantees can be given that the price will not exceed a certain value.

We also look at the convergence rate of the MaxEnt estimation. If it does not converge we, as previously mentioned, fall back to the Norm approach.

3. Results

We study usage time-series data, based on 5-minute snapshots of the aggregated number of PlanetLab slices allocated across the whole network. Data from two months (November-December 2005) were used. Training and future prediction horizons corresponding to predictions roughly from 2 hours to 3 days into the future were evaluated.

3.1. *Modelling*

In Figure 1 we can see that the MaxEnt approximation improves the accuracy of the CDF fit substantially compared to the normal distribution technique. SSE is the sum of the squares of the errors when plotting the

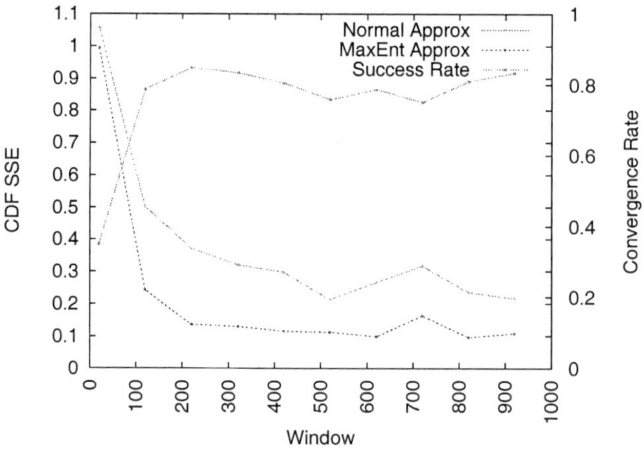

Figure 1. PlanetLab Density Approximation

CDF with a granularity of 100 data points. The windows correspond to number of 5-minute snapshots used to predict the same number of 5-minute snapshots into the future.

We can see that the MaxEnt approximation does not converge in the case of the window size 50 in more than 35% of the cases. We wanted to investigate why, and performed a correlation test on the range of the data values in the window, the standard deviation of the data, and the likelihood of convergence. We obtained correlation coefficients 0.56, and 0.55 for data range and standard deviation respectively which are significant at the 1%-level according to a t-Student test. Intuitively this may be caused by the integral calculations used in the MaxEnt fit being too short to find the underlying entropy maximizing distribution. As a clarification, convergence of the MaxEnt approximation is defined by the error when fitting to the moments expected is less then a certain value ϵ. With the PlanetLab data we saw that an ϵ of 100 worked best, but there is always a tradeoff between accuracy and convergence rate.

3.2. *Predicting the Cumumlative Distribution*

Figure 2 shows an example of an interval estimation and how the different CDF functions compare. The window size in this case was two hours. We can see that the entropy model gives a much better fit to the non-normal behavior of the curve. The histogram estimation (with 100 bins) is quite

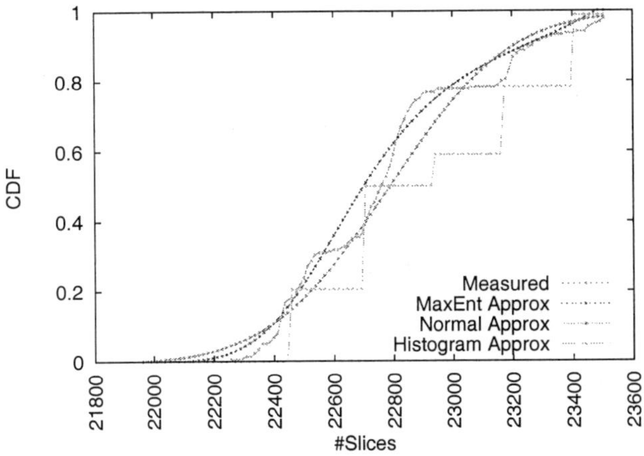

Figure 2. PlanetLab Density Approximation CDF

a coarse grained estimation, and requires more state to be maintained as opposed to just three running moments as in the entropy case.

3.3. *Predicting Bounds*

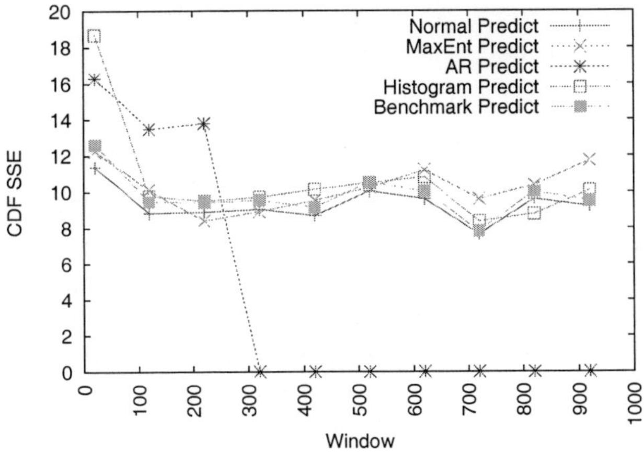

Figure 3. PlanetLab Density Prediction

A bit surprisingly we see in Figure 3 that the MaxEnt model does not produce better prediction results over time than the normal approximation. The AR curve is provided for reference. It does not make sense to use the AR model unless it predicts better than predicting the outcome of the previous period since it also requires all the data points to be kept in history. Since this is not the case for these long-interval predictions it provides no added value in this situation. Another severe limitation of AR is that it numerically due to large Matrix computations is not feasible to predict more than roughly 300 data points into the future. Note that in the graph this is shown by the AR SSE being set to 0 for window sizes greater than 300.

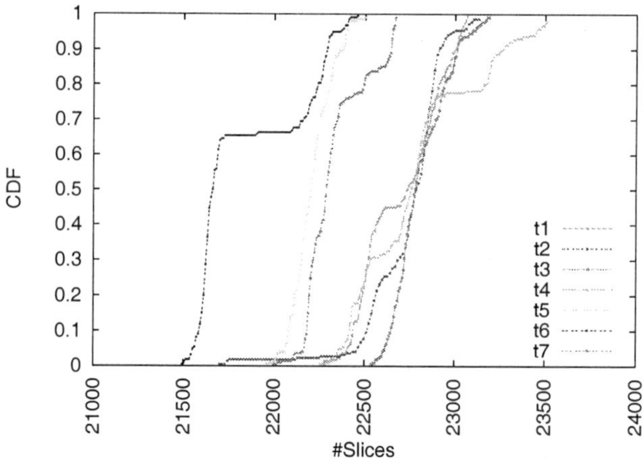

Figure 4. PlanetLab Density Variance

An explanation to why the MaxEnt model cannot benefit from its more accurate density approximations when predicting future densities can be seen in Figure 4. Each CDF in the Figure is taken in a subsequent interval so the t1 curve contains the distribution of all the data points from the start of the measurement to time t1, the t2 curve has all the data points between t1 and t2, etc. The mean point of the density moves back and forth in an unpredictable manner. Another indicator of this is the high SSE value of the benchmark prediction (predicting last periods CDF for the next) in Figure 3 (around 11) compare to the values in 1 (around 0.2).

It is then more encouraging to see that the 99th percentile MaxEnt

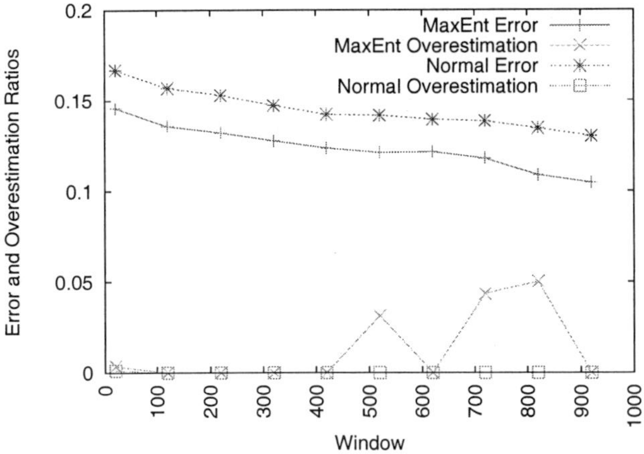

Figure 5. PlanetLab Tail Prediction

estimates in Figure 5 are more accurate than with Norm. We should also note here that the training was done on the maximum amount of history data available and not just the previous period to do more of a worst case estimation of the tail as opposed to an overall accurate one. The error presented in Figure 5 is calculated as the difference between the measured value and the approximation divided by the measured value.

4. Conclusions

Although the statistical prediction algorithms that we examine here were not able to accurately predict future demand in the PlanetLab data set, we found that the MaxEnt algorithm was able to accurately predict bounds on future demand.

Some areas for future work are to examine the performance of MaxEnt in a live system and for systems with different applications and user behaviors than PlanetLab. Ultimately we hope to examine the performance of the algorithms in a live economic Grid system.

Given the fluidity of PlanetLab usage and the lack of a pricing mechanism to moderate usage, the accuracy of the MaxEnt algorithm gives us optimism that prediction algorithms will be accurate in real economic systems. We believe that this will ultimately lead to more stable, more economically efficient systems.

References

1. R. Buyya, D. Abramson, and S. Venugopal. The Grid Economy. *Proceedings of the IEEE, Special Issue on Grid Computing*, 93(3):479–484, March 2005.
2. T. M. Cover and J. A. Thomas. *Elements of Information Theory*. John Wiley & Sons, Inc., 1991.
3. C. A. Cunha, A. Bestavros, and M. E. Crovella. Characteristics of WWW client-based traces. Technical Report TR-95-010, Boston University Department of Computer Science, Apr. 1995. Revised July 18, 1995.
4. David C. Parkes and Ruggiero Cavallo and Nick Elprin and Adam Juda and Sebastien Lahaie and Benjamin Lubin and Loizos Michael and Jeffrey Shneidman and Hassan Sultan. ICE: An Iterative Combinatorial Exchange. In *Proceedings of the ACM Conference on Electronic Commerce*, 2005.
5. E. Jaynes. Information Theory and Statistical Mechanisms. *Physics Review*, 106:620–630, 1957.
6. L. V. Kale, S. Kumar, M. Potnuru, J. DeSouza, and S. Bandhakavi. Faucets: Efficient resource allocation on the computational grid. In *ICPP '04: Proceedings of the 2004 International Conference on Parallel Processing (ICPP'04)*, pages 396–405, Washington, DC, USA, 2004. IEEE Computer Society.
7. K. Lai. Markets are Dead, Long Live Markets. *SIGecom Exchanges*, 5(4):1–10, July 2005.
8. L. Ljung. *System Identification: Theory for the User*. Prentice Hall, December 1998.
9. L. Peterson, T. Anderson, D. Culler, , and T. Roscoe. Blueprint for Introducing Disruptive Technology into the Internet. In *First Workshop on Hot Topics in Networking*, 2002.
10. O. Regev and N. Nisan. The Popcorn Market: Online Markets for Computational Resources. In *Proceedings of 1st International Conference on Information and Computation Economies*, pages 148–157, 1998.
11. C. A. Waldspurger, T. Hogg, B. A. Huberman, J. O. Kephart, and W. S. Stornetta. Spawn: A Distributed Computational Economy. *Software Engineering*, 18(2):103–117, 1992.
12. R. Wolski, J. S. Plank, T. Bryan, and J. Brevik. G-commerce: Market formulations controlling resource allocation on the computational grid. In *IPDPS '01: Proceedings of the 15th International Parallel and Distributed Processing Symposium (IPDPS'01)*, page 10046.2, Washington, DC, USA, 2001. IEEE Computer Society.
13. X. Wu and T. Stengos. Partially adaptive estimation via the maximum entropy densities. *Econometrics Journal*, 8(3):352–366, 2005.
14. L. Xiao, Y. Zhu, L. M. Ni, and Z. Xu. Gridis: An incentive-based grid scheduling. In *IPDPS '05: Proceedings of the 19th IEEE International Parallel and Distributed Processing Symposium (IPDPS'05) - Papers*, page 65.2, Washington, DC, USA, 2005. IEEE Computer Society.

EXPERIMENTAL AND EMPIRICAL PERSPECTIVES ON GRID RESOURCE ALLOCATION FOR THE SINGAPORE MARKET

DANNY OH, STEVEN MILLER, HU NAN

School of Information Systems
Singapore Management University, Singapore

In this paper, we describe our work on using the Tycoon system developed by HP Labs to provide a market-based resource allocation and bidding framework for a grid. We discuss how we intend to evaluate the feasibility of the Tycoon system by measuring its economic performance using agent-based simulation experiments for a particular type of grid usage scenario, namely, the digital media market scenario. We will also discuss a related effort in collecting and using real grid data from the National Grid Pilot Platform in Singapore and how we will be using real data collected to derive actual usage patterns to verify the demand models used in the experiments. Lastly, we discuss the impact and significance of our work in the design and execution of commercialized grid business models for the digital media grid market hub.

1. Introduction

Accenture [1] notes there are six major technologies which are evolving to form the foundations for realizing the vision of utility computing:

- Grid Computing
- Workload Management and Virtualization
- Web Security
- Data Center Automation
- Autonomic Computing
- Blade Computing

In this paper, we describe our work on using the Tycoon system developed by HP Labs [19, 20, 21] to provide a market-based resource allocation and bidding framework for a grid. This work is a part of a larger effort in Singapore to provide grid technology applications and business models needed to support the emergence of a grid market hub where IT services can be provided to and purchased by a community of digital media users in a utility computing framework. Thus, this paper is focusing on one approach for incorporating a market-based resource allocation and bidding framework into the larger workload management infrastructure of a grid.

2. Motivation

We evaluate the feasibility of the Tycoon system by measuring its economic performance using agent-based simulation experiments for a particular type of grid usage scenario, namely the digital media market scenario. We are exploring how Tycoon operates under various market conditions for this market scenario. We are using both experimental and empirical methods to gain insights into how we can design feasible and practical market-based resource allocation models for a digital media grid market. We are also exploring the limitations of the Tycoon system, in order to determine how to enhance the Tycoon framework or how to create policies or other measures to overcome the limitations.

3. Related Work for the Experimental Analysis

The key advantage of approaching resource allocation from an economics perspective is that it provides incentives for resource providers to participate in the grid as they are able to charge consumers "credits" for the use of IT resources. Resources are always limited and cannot be free for use or we will risk running into the "tragedy of the commons" problem [11]. Moreover, the market-based approach sets the stage for organizations to establish a pay-per-use model for IT services within their data centers and eventually allows for the trading of IT services in a grid market hub. Another advantage is that it allows researchers to draw upon a large body of economics and management science research that can be related to emerging grid markets, resource allocation and business models.

The main types of market-based resource allocation models that have been studied in the context of grid computing are:

- auction models [4, 8, 9, 19, 20, 21, 24, 27]
- bid-based proportional share models [4, 10, 15]
- commodity market models [12, 16, 28, 31, 32, 33, 36]
- tendering/contract-net models [25, 34]
- community/coalition/bartering models [26]

Of these, the auction-based model appears to be the most widely studied type. Overviews of auction mechanisms are provided by Buyya et al. [29, 30] (as applied to grid computing as of 2002) and by Parkes et al. [19] (as applied to auctions in general as of 2003). Parkes et al. also illustrate the role of theoretical mechanism design in the design of auctions and exchanges for electronic markets.

Potential benefits can be gained from automating markets. For example in a Tycoon-based market, agents could perform the laborious task of monitoring whether the resource allocation has dropped below certain threshold, and if it does, help users to increase the bid. An overview of how agents and grid technologies can advance and support each other can be found in [14]. Wellman et al. [18] study the issues in the design of automated markets with software agents.

The following papers by Kenyon et al. discuss the general issues on grid resource commercialization. In [6], Kenyon et al. provide a conceptual framework for grid resource commercialization. In [11], from past research in the financial and commodity markets, Kenyon et al. outline the lessons learnt in the long history of asset management and decision-support for these markets and shows the relevance of these lessons for grid commercialization.

Existing bodies of work on Tycoon can be found in [20, 21, 23] We note two additional auction model research efforts that provide capabilities that are know to be limitations of the current Tycoon system. One interesting auction study [13] in the context of pricing for on-demand computing services is the contingent auction whereby users bid for computing resources in an auction, but are partially refunded if demand is not realized. Tycoon currently does not support the refund of credits for jobs that fail. The strategyproofness of an auction mechanism for dynamic resource allocation is also important in the grid environments such as the grid market hub. Parkes et al. describe in [7] the Virtual World mechanism which removes any incentive for a resource provider to overstate its available capacity (in order to get more bidders) and provides insights on how the resource provider can understate its capacity and increase its payments. Tycoon currently does not claim to be strategyproof. We will discuss Tycoon in more detail in the next section.

4. Experimental View of Grid Resource Allocation using Tycoon

4.1. *Overview of the Tycoon System*

Tycoon is a market-based resource allocation system which allows users to bid and pay for resources using credits. Tycoon uses an open source virtualization tool called Xen [35] to create a virtualized layer between applications and the underlying hardware resources. In this way, Tycoon, through Xen, captures a uniform snapshot of the IT environment and connects IT resources that have been historically separated. Tycoon functions on top of this virtualized platform to help manage and provision hardware resources and continuously balance workloads through a Tycoon grid.

Each Tycoon host runs an auction share scheduler which listens to request for bids from clients and holds continuous bid auctions to determine resource allocation. Bid requests are specified in terms of constraints such as the amount of credits to spend and the deadline for job completion. These constraints can be changed while the job is running. The bid is computed as the pricing rate that the user will pay for the required job execution time. Both time and cost QoS attributes are considered. The request with the highest bid is then allocated the largest processor, memory and disk time slice, and the request with the second highest bid is allocated the second largest processor, memory and disk time slice, etc. Once the bid is accepted by a host, the auction share scheduler will instantiate a new Xen virtual machine to run the job. It will also perform the necessary setup and configuration to run the job. Once the staging of the job is completed, the job will be run immediately at the host. While the number of virtual hosts is less than the maximum number of virtual hosts allowable per physical host, the auctioneer will continue to listen for bids. And whenever a new bid is accepted, the auctioneer will recalculate the resource allocation share for each running job at regular intervals.

The continuous bidding auction mechanism provides a means to solicit true user valuations for resources and it allows for more efficient resource allocation. It also enables adaptive resource allocation as new requests will modify and reduce the current resource allocations of existing executing requests. However, this could have a negative impact on risk-averse and latency-sensitive applications. One possible solution would be to implement resource reservation to secure resource entitlements in advance. However, Tycoon currently does not handle resource reservation.

For resource management, Tycoon adopts a decentralized approach as each host self-manages its own set of local applications. Using virtual machines, multiple applications can be concurrently executed. Basic accounting information is kept in each host so that the usage-based service cost to be paid by the user can be calculated.

Simulation results for performance evaluation [20, 21, 23] show that the Tycoon is able to achieve high fairness and low latency as compared to simple proportional-share strategy. Resource acquisition is also fast and limited only by communication delays. It also does not impose any manual bidding overhead on users. Moreover, the Tycoon resource allocation algorithm is relatively simple and it allows for the fast multiplexing of resources on a host.

Additionally, Tycoon has demonstrated how communication and management overheads could be minimized in the design of auction mechanism.

For example, the continuous bidding auctions are held internally within each host and this reduces communication across hosts.

4.2. *Experimental Objectives*

The purpose of our experiments is to evaluate Tycoon's suitability to be deployed as a resource allocation and bidding mechanism in the digital media market scenario. To do so, we will measure its economic performance under several market conditions.

4.3. *Design of the Tycoon Simulation Experiments*

We will adopt an agent-based approach for the design and implementation of the simulation experiments. Software agents will be used to simulate actual users competing for resources on a particular Tycoon host.

Table 1 provides an overview of the experiment setup.

System Configuration
• 2 Intel servers running Fedora Core 4 and Xen 3.
• 1 server installed as Tycoon host and 1 server as Tycoon client.
• 5 agents running on Tycoon client and submitting jobs to Tycoon host.
Rationale
• Tycoon works at node-level and not cluster-level. Therefore, it is sufficient to use only 1 Tycoon host for the experiment.
Sample Workload Related to digital media
• Blender rendering software.
• 100-frame rendering job.
Rationale
• We have chosen the Blender rendering software as it is a widely used open-source rendering tool by the digital media community.
Demand Patterns
Pattern 1: Equal Load
• Rendering jobs of same duration submitted at regular intervals.
Pattern 2: Bursty Load
• Long rendering jobs submitted at the start of the simulation run.
• Short rendering jobs submitted at pre-determined intervals.
Pattern 3: Increasing Load
• Rendering jobs with increasing durations submitted at regular intervals.
Pattern 4: Decreasing Load
• Rendering jobs with decreasing durations submitted at regular intervals.

Simulation Protocol
• Run simulation experiments for each job distribution and for different bidding behaviours (i.e. willingness to change bid). • Before running the experiments, run a single instance of the 100-frame rendering job to determine the performance level (in CPU MHz) needed. • To start simulation, agent determines the expected job completion time (bid interval in seconds) for the given performance level. • Agent determines the expected credits to be spent (bid amount in $) for the given performance level and job completion time. • Agent determines the available hosts and select one host. • Agent submits the bid to the selected host. • Host performs the necessary setup to run the job if bid is successful. • While job is running, agent records and logs the following job information at regular intervals: ❖ Current share of resources allocated (CPU, memory and disk). ❖ Current bid amount. ❖ Current bid interval. ❖ New bid amount. ❖ New bid interval. ❖ Funds remaining. ❖ Time lapsed in seconds since job was started. ❖ Number of frames rendered.
Analysis of Simulation Results
• Based on the simulation data collected, we want to determine the following: • Utility ❖ Defined as cost ($) per throughput. ❖ Throughout is defined as total number of frames of the rendering job. • Efficiency ❖ Defined as the sum of utilities for all users across all time intervals. • Total Credits Used ❖ Defined as the number of credits actually used to complete the job. • Additional Funding ❖ Defined as the number of additional credits needed to fund the account so that job can be completed. • Total Time Taken for Job Completion ❖ Defined as the number of seconds taken for a job to be completed.

4.4. *Impacts and Contributions of Analysis*

From our initial study of Tycoon, the continuous bidding strategy has some inherent limitations. Even though Lai et al. [21] claim that users do not need to spend time to monitor their bids, we believe that users would need to frequently monitor the amount of resources allocated to their jobs. This is especially true if there is high resource competition on the host. The reason is that a user with a very large bid can potentially take over the entire system resources of the host. The other running jobs may potentially be halted due to insufficient resources. This problem cannot be resolved by transferring the job to another host as Tycoon currently does not support this.

In addition, users with high priority jobs may not accept the continuous bidding strategy as there is no guarantee that their jobs will be completed after they have spent an initial amount of credits. They may need to spend more credits to get their jobs to be completed eventually if there is resource constraint on the host.

One possible solution is to build bidding agents that help users automate the continuous bidding process. The agents can increase the bid amount if the resources allocated falls below a certain threshold. Similarly, if too much resources are allocated, the agents can help users to save credits by decreasing the bid amount.

From the simulation results, we hope to gain more insights into the construction of an agent-mediated digital media grid market hub that uses Tycoon-like mechanisms for resource allocation and bidding.

5. Related Work for the Empirical Analysis

Published studies based on PlanetLab such as those by Chun et al. [2, 3] provide an empirical analysis of large data sets from federated distributed computational and communication infrastructures. These studies present detailed characterization of the actual use of the PlanetLab testbed in terms of the quantity and patterns of usage of network, CPU, memory and disk resources. Peterson et al. [22] have noted the difference between PlanetLab and a grid. Despite these differences, the concerns of PlanetLab and grids are converging, and we think that the empirical studies of resource usage in the PlanetLab settings should be carefully studied to provide guidance on what to expect in Grid settings.

6. Empirical View of Grid Resource Allocation in the National Grid Pilot Platform (NGPP)

6.1. *Empirical Objectives*

From the empirical analysis of the NGPP dataset, we aim to discover demand patterns that we can use to understand user behaviour in grid usage. We also can use the analysis results to verify and fine tune the demand patterns used for the simulation. If we can understand user behaviour in grid usage, for example, understand why certain nodes were used and why certain costs were paid, we could create better demand models and incorporate such preferences into the agents so as to run more realistic and accurate simulation experiments.

6.2. *Design of the Analysis Strategy of NGPP Dataset*

We will adopt a time-series analysis for the analysis and visualization of the NGPP dataset. Data will be analyzed and visualized in different ways, for example, in terms of big task vs small task and in terms of the nature of the task.

We will also be examining the following distributions:

- Distribution of the job (frequency vs. cumulative frequency).
- Distribution of the length of each job (frequency vs. cumulative frequency).
- Distribution of the normalized CPU/memory/disk usage per job.
- Distribution of credits paid per job.

From these distributions, we will use regression techniques and correlation matrices to derive the actual demand patterns in terms of the job structure and composition, and job quantity and distribution over time.

6.3. *Challenges of collecting a Grid Dataset*

A major challenge in gaining access to the NGPP dataset was to obtain the formal permissions from all of the resource providers to access the grid information. The NGPP user community is understandably very concerned about the security and privacy of the information. They do not want information on individual users to be revealed. To address the security and privacy concerns, we created and signed a non-disclosure agreement with each relevant organization contributing to or using the NGPP resources and we have also developed a filtering program to mask out user information before the data extraction. Working through the administrative issues to address the security and privacy concerns and to execute the non-disclosure agreements took about one year.

7. Reaching for Insights on Real World Market-Based Resource Allocation

Many research efforts conducted by grid technology and management science researchers have concentrated on analyzing the efficiency or optimality of their resource allocation algorithms. Most of this prior work has not evolved to the stage of testing the algorithms using real world data sets or market situations. As we note, it is a challenging task for researchers to obtain access to real world data sets and market situations. We are pursuing a two-pronged approach of exploring the capabilities of the Tycoon resource allocation mechanism via the simulation of a digital media market scenario, and in parallel collecting and analyzing real grid data to understand patterns of resource usage. We believe this effort will help to bridge the gap between prior theoretical and experimental work and current and emerging needs to create practical market-based resource allocation models that can be used as the foundation for grid marketplaces where individual providers can construct business models that will make their services attractive to prospective users.

This research is currently underway. We are implementing the proposed agent-based grid simulator for Tycoon on a Java platform and investigating the economic performance of Tycoon via simulation experiments of a digital media market scenario.

8. Conclusion

In this contribution, we have discussed how we intend to evaluate the feasibility of the Tycoon system by measuring its economic performance using agent-based simulation experiments for a particular type of grid usage scenario, namely, the digital media market scenario. We have also discussed a related but separate effort in collecting and using real grid data from the National Grid Pilot Platform in Singapore and how we will be using the data collected to verify the usage patterns used in the simulation. Lastly, we have outlined the impact and significance of our work in the design of feasible and practical market-based resource allocation models for a digital media grid market hub.

Acknowledgement

This work is supported by the Adaptive Enterprise @ Singapore Technology Alliance Scheme of the Infocomm Development Authority of Singapore and by the School of Information Systems, Singapore Management University.

References

1. Accenture, "Utility Computing: The Future State of the High-Performance IT Infrastructure", Technical Report, 2004.
2. A. AuYoung, B. N. Chun, A. C. Snoeren, and A. Vahdat, "Resource Allocation in Federated Distributed Computing Infrastructures", Proc. of the 1st Workshop on Operating System and Architectural Support for the On-Demand IT Infrastructure, 2004.
3. B. Chun, and A. Vahdat, "Workload and Failure Characterization on a Large-Scale Federated Testbed", Intel Research, IRB-TR-03-040, Nov. 12, 2003.
4. B. Chun, and D. Culler, "Market-Based Proportional Resource Sharing for Clusters", University of California, Berkeley, Missouri, USA, Technical Report CSD-1092, Jan. 2000.
5. B. Cooper, and H. Garcia-Molina, "Bidding for Storage Space in a Peer-to-Peer Data Preservation System", Proc. of the 22nd Int. Conf. on Distributed Computing Systems (ICDSC 2002), Vienna, Austria, Jul. 2-5, 2002.
6. C. Kenyon, and G. Cheliotis, "Grid Resource Commercialization: Economic Engineering and Delivery Scenarios", Grid Resource Management: State of the Art and Research Issues, Editors: J. Nabrzyski, J. Schopf and J. Weglarz, Kluwer, 2003.
7. C. Ng, D. C. Parkes, and M. Seltzer, "Virtual Worlds: Fast and Strategyproof Auctions for Dynamic Resource Allocation", Proc. of the 4th ACM Conf. on Electronic Commerce (EC'03), pages 238-239, 2003.
8. C. S. Yeo, and R. Buyya, "A Taxonomy of Market-based Resource Management Systems for Utility-driven Cluster Computing", Software: Practice and Experience (SPE) Journal, Wiley Press, USA (in print, accepted in Sept. 2005).
9. C. Waldspurger, T. Hogg, B. Huberman, J. Kephart, and W. Stornetta, "Spawn: A Distributed Computational Economy", IEEE Trans. Softw. Eng., vol. 18, no. 2, pp. 103–117, Feb. 1992.
10. D. Reed, I. Pratt, P. Menage, S. Early, and N. Stratford, "Xenoservers: Accounted Execution of Untrusted Code", presented at the 7th Workshop Hot Topics in Operating Systems (HotOS-VII), Rio Rico, AZ, Mar. 28–30, 1999.
11. G. Cheliotis, C. Kenyon, and R. Buyya, "10 Lessons from Finance for Commercial Sharing of IT Resources", Peer-to-Peer Computing: The Evolution of a Disruptive Technology, Idea Group Publishing, ch 11, pp 244-264, 2005.
12. G. Heiser, F. Lam, and S. Russell, "Resource Management in the Mungi Single-address-space Operating System", presented at the Australasian Computer Science Conf., Perth, Australia, Feb. 4-6, 1998.
13. H. K. Bhargava, and S. Sundaresan, "Computing as Utility: Managing Availability, Commitment and Pricing through Contingent Bid Auctions", Journal of Management Information Systems, Vol. 50, Issue 3, Fall 2004.
14. I. Foster, N.R. Jennings, and C. Kesselman, "Brain meets Brawn: Why Grid and Agents need each other", Proc. of the 3rd Int. Conf. on Autonomous Agents and Multiagent Systems (AAMAS), 2004.
15. J. Bredin, D. Kotz, and D. Rus, "Utility Driven Mobile-Agent Scheduling. Dartmouth College", Hanover, NH, Tech. Rep. CS-TR98-331, Oct. 3, 1998.
16. J. Brooke, M. Foster, S. Pickles, K. Taylor, and T. Hewitt, "Minigrids: Effective Test-Beds for Grid Application", presented at the 1st IEEE/ACM Int. Workshop Grid Computing (GRID 2000), Bangalore, India, Dec. 17, 2000.
17. J. Gomoluch, and M. Schroeder, "Market-based Allocation for Grid Computing: A Model and Simulation", in the Int. Middleware Conf., Workshop Proc, PUC-Rio, pp 211-218, 2003.
18. J. K. MacKie-Mason, and M. P. Wellman, "Automated Markets and Trading Agents", Handbook of Computational Economics, Vol. 2: Agent-Based Computational Economics, Leigh Tesfatsion and Kenneth L. Judd (eds.), North-Holland, 2006.
19. J. Kalagnanam, and D. C. Parkes, "Auctions, Bidding and Exchange Design", in Simchi-Levi, Wu, Shen: Supply Chain Analysis in the eBusiness Area, Kluwer Academic Publishers, 2003.

20. K. Lai, B. A. Huberman, and L. Fine, "Tycoon: A Distributed Market-based Resource Allocation Systems", Technical Report, Hewlett Packard, April 5, 2004.
21. K. Lai, L. Rasmusson, E. Adar, S. Sorkin, L. Zhang, and B. A. Huberman, "Tycoon: An Implementation of a Distributed Market-Based Resource Allocation System", Technical Report, Hewlett Packard, Dec. 8, 2004.
22. L. Peterson, T. Anderson, D. Culler, and T. Roscoe, "A Blueprint for Introducing Disruptive Technology into the Internet", Proc. of the 1st ACM Workshop on Hot Topics in Networks, Princeton, NJ, October, 2002.
23. M. Feldman, K. Lai, and L. Zhang, "A Price Anticipating Resource Allocation Mechanism for Distributed Shared Clusters", Proc. of the 6th ACM conference on Electronic Commerce, ACM press, pp 127-136, 2005.
24. M. Frank (2002, Apr.), "The OCEAN Project: The Open Computation Exchange & Auctioning Network", [online], available: http://www.cise.ufl.edu/research/ocean/
25. M. Stonebraker, R. Devine, M. Kornacker, W. Litwin, A. Pfeffer, A. Sah, and C. Staelin, "An Economic Paradigm for Query Processing and Data Migration in Mariposa", in the 3rd Int. Conf. Parallel and Distributed Information Systems, Austin, TX, Sep. 28-30, 1994.
26. Mojo Nation (2006, Mar.), [online], available: http://mnetproject.org/
27. O. Regev, and N. Nisan, "The POPCORN Market - An Online Market for Computational Resources", Proc. of the 1st Int. Conf. on Information and Computation Economies, ACM Press, pp 148-157, 1998.
28. R. Buyya, D. Abramson, and J. Giddy, "Nimrod-G: An Architecture for a Resource Management and Scheduling System in a Global Computational Grid", presented at the 4th Int. Conf. High Performance Computing in Asia-Pacific Region (HPC Asia 2000), Beijing, China, May 2000.
29. R. Buyya, D. Abramson, and S. Venugopal, "The Grid Economy", Proc. of the IEEE, Volume 93, Issue 3, pp 698-714, 2005.
30. R. Buyya, D. Abramson, J. Giddy, and H. Stockinger, "Economic Models for Resource Management and Scheduling in Grid Computing", Concurrency and Computation: Practice and Experience (14), pp 1507-1542, 2002.
31. R. Buyya, and S. Vazhkudai, "Compute Power Market: Towards a Market-Oriented Grid", presented in the 1st IEEE/ACM Int. Symposium on Cluster Computing and the Grid (CCGrid 2001), 2001.
32. R. Wolski, J. Brevik, J. Plank, and T. Bryan, "Grid Resource Allocation and Control using Computational Economies", in Grid Computing: Making the Global Infrastructure a Reality, pages 747-772. Wiley and Sons, 2003.
33. R. Wolski, J. Plank, J. Brevik, and T. Bryan, "Analyzing Market-based Resource Allocation Strategies for the Computational Grid", the Int. Journal of High Performance Computing Applications, pages 258-281, 2001.
34. S. Lalis, and A. Karipidis, "An Open Market-based Framework for Distributed Computing over the Internet", in the 1st IEEE/ACM Int. Workshop Grid Computing (GRID 2000), Bangalore, India, Dec. 17, 2000.
35. Xen Hypervisor (2006, Mar.), available: http://www.xensource.com
36. Y. Amir, B. Awerbuch, A. Barak, S. Borgstrom, and A. Keren, "An Opportunity Cost Approach for Job Assignment in a Scalable Computing Cluster", IEEE Trans. Parallel Distributed System, Jul. 2000, vol. 11, pp. 760-768.

AN EVALUATION OF COMMUNICATION DEMAND OF AUCTION PROTOCOLS IN GRID ENVIRONMENTS

MARCOS DIAS DE ASSUNÇÃO AND RAJKUMAR BUYYA

Grid Computing and Distributed Systems Laboratory and NICTA Victoria Laboratory
Department of Computer Science and Software Engineering
The University of Melbourne, Victoria, 3053, Australia
http://www.gridbus.org

Dynamic pricing and good level of Pareto optimality make auctions more attractive for resource allocation over other economic models. However, some auction models present drawbacks regarding the high demand of communication when applied to large-scale scenarios. In a complex Grid environment, the communication demand can become a bottleneck; that is, a number of messages need to be exchanged for matching suitable service providers and consumers. In this context, it is worthwhile to investigate the communication demand or complexity of auction protocols in Grid environments. This work presents an analysis on the communication requirements of four auction protocols, namely First-Price Sealed, English, Dutch, and Continuous double auctions, in Grid environments. In addition, we provide a framework supporting auction protocols within a Grid simulating toolkit called GridSim.

1. Introduction

Grid computing [1] came along from the need to utilize globally distributed computing and storage resources in a networked environment for solving large-scale problems in science, engineering and commerce. This technology is also considered a key enabler for creation of cyberinfrastructure required for e-Science [2] and e-Business [3] applications.

However, one of the key challenges with grid computing technology is the efficient and sustained sharing and management of resources. To that end, the area of microeconomics provides a source of ideas. This is done on the notion that: (i) Grid resources are priced and charging for their use can provide incentives for resource providers to share their resources. (ii) The economic behavior of consumers and providers defines how to allocate resources. In applying economic methods to this problem, one must take into account factors such as pricing of resources and its relationship with supply and demand.

In an auction, an auctioneer wants to allocate a good, whereas bidders or market participants bid reflecting their desire in taking the good. The auctioneer decides to whom allocate the item by using an auction algorithm to find the best bid. Auctions provide a method for determining prices based on bidders' bids, which reflect demand, and owners' reserve prices, which reflect supply abundance or scarcity [4][5]. This way, auctions simplify the allocation problem by summarizing the bidder's wishes and owners' offers in terms of price.

Auctioning models are a source of solutions to the challenge of resource allocation in Grid because they provide a decentralized structure, are easier to implement than other economic models and respect the autonomy of resource owners. The dynamic nature of the Grid requires mechanisms where resource users and owners can agree upon the amount of resources they will use and the price paid for them. Auctions allow owners and users to establish prices to resources in the Grid and guarantee social efficiency in resource allocations. However, auctions present some drawbacks regarding the demand they place on communication i.e., interactions involved in negotiation of service price. In a complex Grid environment, the communication requirements of some auction models may become a bottleneck. Thus, it is important to analyze such economic models from a communication complexity perspective in order to identify the requirements of different auction protocols when applied to Grid environments.

In this work, we investigate the communication requirements of four auction protocols in Grid environments, namely First-Price Sealed-Bid, English, Dutch and Continuous double auctions. Since the amount of information carried by messages in auctions varies with different scenarios, we measure the number of messages exchanged and then identify the suitability of each strategy to Grid computing in terms of communication complexity. In addition, we contribute towards the development of a framework for realizing auction protocols in the GridSim simulator [6], which simplifies the task of development and evaluation of auction models for resource management under different scenarios in simulated Grid environments.

The rest of the paper is organized as follows. We present the motivations as well as background ideas in Section 2. Section 3 presents a description of the framework for the simulation of auction protocols in GridSim. Section 4 contains a brief discussion of the auction protocols analyzed in this paper. Simulation environment and experimental results are presented in Section 5. Section 6 concludes the paper along with thoughts on future work.

2. Motivations and Related Work

In the literature, we find several works applying auction models for resource management in distributed computing systems. However, there is a need for investigating their suitability for Grid computing as it presents a dynamic and large-scale computing environment for sharing resources distributed across multiple administrative domains [7]. Such analysis can take into account several criterions such as social efficiency, equilibrium and complexity of auction protocols. Another important study is on their requirements of communication when applied to Grid environments.

Grosu and Das [8] present an analysis of First-Price auction, Vickrey auction and Double auction. The work in [11] presents an analysis of three different Double auction protocols. The aim of these works is to analyze the suitability of auction protocols to resource allocation in Grids; the analysis is performed from the perspective of both users and providers. Experimental results support that First-Price auctions favor providers, Vickrey auctions favor users, and Double auctions favor both. The analysis takes into account user payments, resource profits, and resource utilization. The work in [5] presents a series of factors to consider when choosing an auction model to use. The auction mechanisms taken into account comprise the receiving of bids, the manner in which information is revealed and its quantity, and how the auction is cleared. Mathias *et al.* [9] use an approach similar to the one present in this work, in which a broker is the auctioneer and resources are the bidders that bid for the execution of jobs. The performance of a First-Price sealed auction is measured considering queue time, runtime, and makespan. However, none of these works consider the demand of communication and its complexity.

Shen *et al.* [10] propose an adaptive negotiation approach for Grid computing. By following this approach, the system can adapt to computation needs by changing the models currently in use. In this regard, communication could be one of the factors used to alternate from a model to another. In this context, it will be interesting to investigate the communication requirements of different auction models, which agents can take into account when choosing a suitable protocol.

3. Design of the Auction Framework

The main participants in an auction are the seller, the auctioneer and the buyers. Figure 1 presents an example of reverse auction for Grid computing in which users are buyers, brokers are auctioneers and resource providers are sellers. In reverse auctions, the buyer starts the auction and the sellers bid to sell a service to the buyer. In such a case, a Dutch auction becomes ascending. Hereafter, we use the terms users to buyers, auctioneer to refer to the broker and bidders to resource providers. Although we use reverse auctions in this paper, the framework is generic and provides means for normal auctions to be conducted on behalf of service providers.

Initially, the user submits jobs to her broker. In the Grid, a broker is responsible for submitting, managing and monitoring the execution of jobs on the user's behalf. The broker creates an auction and sets additional parameters of the auction such as job length, the number of auction rounds, the reserve price and the policy to be used (e.g. English, Dutch or any other auction policy implemented by the user). As the broker also plays the role of auctioneer, it posts the auction to itself; otherwise, the auction would be posted to an external auctioneer. The auctioneer informs the bidders that a Dutch auction is about to start. Then, the auctioneer creates a call for proposals (CFP), sets its initial price, and broadcasts the CFP to all the bidders. Resource providers formulate bids for selling a service to the user to execute her job. In the example, at the first time that bidders evaluate the CFP, they decide not to bid because the price offered is below what they are willing to charge for the service. This leads the auctioneer to increase the price and send a new CFP with the new price. This process continues until a bidder who is willing to accept the offer made by the auctioneer makes a bid. In the example, a bidder decides to bid in the second round. The auctioneer clears the auction according to the Dutch policy specified beforehand. Once the auction clears, it informs the outcome to the user and the bidders.

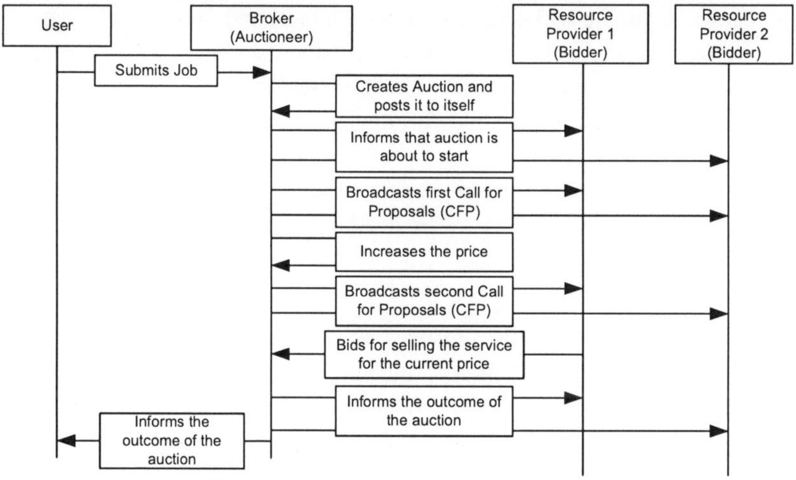

Figure 1. General view of our auction model.

Based on this model of auctions, we have designed and implemented a generalized auction framework that allows users to develop and evaluate auction protocols for resource management in Grids by using GridSim Grid simulator.

The main classes that compose the auction framework are (Figure 2):

- **Auctioneer:** This class extends GridSim entity and implements the basic behavior of an auctioneer. An auctioneer may involve in multiple auctions, send call for proposals, receive bids, maintain a list of the auctions, and remove them when they clear.
- **Auction:** An auction contains attributes that are common to every auction.
- **OneSidedAuction:** This class extends Auction and defines methods for auctions that accept only bids, unlike double auctions that accept asks and bids.

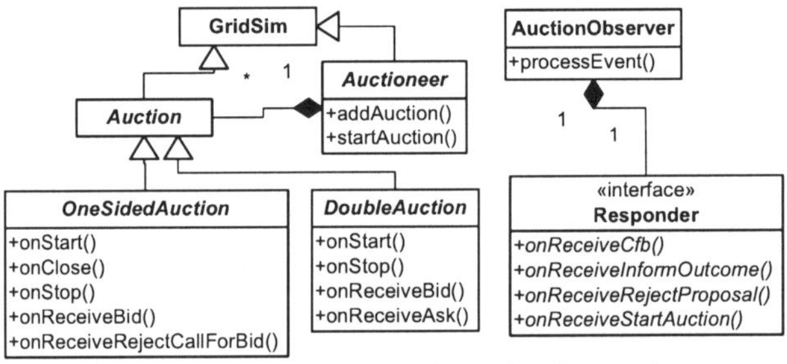

Figure 2. A class diagram of the auction framework.

- **DoubleAuction:** This abstract class defines the basic behavior for a double auction. A double auction accepts asks and bids, and tries to match them.
- **AuctionObserver:** To participate in auctions, a bidder uses an observer. The bidder forwards messages to her AuctionObserver. The observer has a responder that is responsible for implementing the bidder's side of the auction.
- **Responder:** A class that implements this interface defines the bidder's policy and deals with messages received during the auction process.

4. Auction Protocols

This section presents a brief overview of the auction protocols examined in this work. In the description of these protocols, we consider that the auction is conducted on behalf of the seller. These auction protocols include:

English Auction (EA): This [12] is an ascending auction in which the auctioneer tries to find the price of a good by proposing an initial price below the supposed market value and slowly raising the price until no bidder is interested in paying the current price for the good. Then the best past bid is chosen.

Dutch Auction (DA): This [12] is a descending auction and differs from the English auction in the sense that the auctioneer starts by issuing a call for proposals with a price much higher than the expected market value. The auctioneer then gradually decreases the price until some bidder shows interest in taking the good for the price announced.

First-Price Sealed Auction (FPSA): In our implementation of the First-Price sealed auction, bidders are not aware of each other's offers. In addition, it is a single round auction. When bidders receive a call for proposals, they can verify the minimum price and either decide to bid or not to bid for the good. The auctioneer waits a given time for the bids and then allocates the good to the bidder who has valued the good the most.

Continuous Double Auction (CDA): The Continuous double auction [13] works with a system of bids and asks. The price is found by matching asks and bids. The auctioneer accepts asks and bids and tries to match them. The auctioneer informs the price to the bidder and the seller when a match is made.

5. Simulation Environment and Experimental Results

Our experiments consider that auctions are all-to-all; that is, all auctioneers send messages to all possible bidders in the Grid. In our first simulation, a user submits applications (jobs) to her broker, which in turn initiates an auction for each job, similar to the example presented in the Section 3. We use reverse auctions here. Therefore, resource providers are the bidders and they bid for executing jobs. Since the auctioneer tries to find the lowest bid, an English auction becomes descending (with the auctioneer sending call for bids with the price set to the maximum amount of budget allocated to the task) while a Dutch auction becomes ascending (starting with the initial price set to the minimum amount of budget allocated to the task). The First-Price sealed auction starts with the announced price set to the maximum budget provided to the task whereas the auctioneer allocates the job to the provider that has made the lowest bid.

We simulated configurations of 1, 5, 10, 20, 30, 40 and 50 resources, each with 1000 MIPS (million instructions per second) processing capacity. The configurations have 2, 10, 20, 40, 60, 80 and 100 users respectively. The cost per second of CPU is uniformly distributed from 5 to 10. The limit of auction rounds for English and Dutch is set to 10 and each round with timeout of 1 minute. The First-Price sealed auction has only one round. Each user generates 10 jobs uniformly distributed in an interval of 5 hours. The job length follows a uniform distribution from 2000 to 5000 MIs (Millions of Instructions). A user receives a budget uniformly distributed between 300 and 900 to spend with the execution of jobs. We consider that a user wishes to spend from a minimum of 10% to a maximum of 100% of this budget to have her jobs executed. To choose the price paid to execute a job, the user utilizes her budged proportional to the length of the jobs.

A bidder (resource provider) bids depending on the job length and auction scenario. The bidder evaluates the cost to execute the job and applies an expected marginal profit that follows a uniform distribution from 1% to 50%. The bidder decides to bid if the price announced by the auctioneer is greater than the sum of her cost and marginal profit. In English and Dutch auctions, the price set in the bid is the price announced by the auctioneer whereas in First-Price sealed and Continuous double auctions, the price inserted into the bid is the price initially estimated by the bidder.

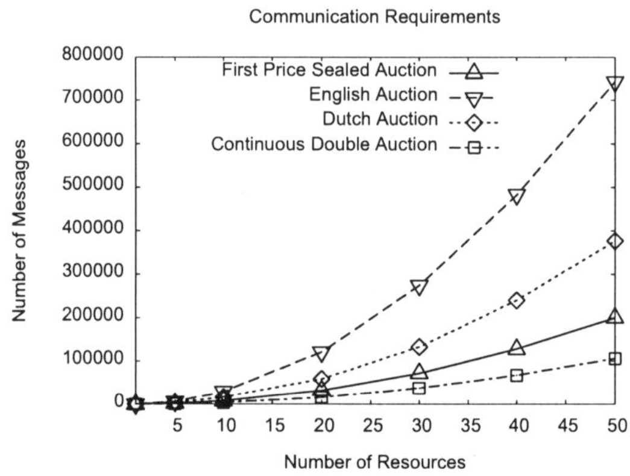

Figure 3. The communication demand of different protocols.

In Continuous double auctions, the auctioneer matches asks and bids. The auctioneer maintains a list of asks ordered in a decreasing order and a list of bids ordered in an increasing order. When the auctioneer receives an ask she proceeds as follows:

1. She compares it with the first bid of the list. If the price in the ask is greater than or equal to the bid's value, it informs that seller and bidder can trade at the price (`price ask + price bid) / 2`)
2. Otherwise, the auctioneer adds the ask in the list.

If the auctioneer receives a bid, she does the following:

1. She compares it with the first ask of the list. If the price in the ask is greater than or equal to the bid's value, it informs that seller and bidder can trade at the price (`price ask + price bid) / 2`).
2. Otherwise, the auctioneer adds the bid in the list.

Figure 3 shows the number of messages exchanged for the different configurations of resources in each kind of auction. Figure 4 presents the number of messages grouped by category when the environment has 30 resources and 60 users. The English auction is the model that involves the greatest number of messages, followed by the Dutch auction. The First-Price Sealed auction model presents less requirements of communication mainly because it has just one round. The protocol that performs better and has less communication demand is the Continuous double auction. The English auction model presents a higher number of messages because multiple bidders can bid in a single round, even though it considers only the first bid in each round and discards the others. The Dutch auction presents fewer messages because bidders do not bid while they are not interested in the price. The performance of the English auction is also related to the starting price and the price setting mechanism because it may start at a price very distant from the final one and can take several rounds to achieve it. We notice that the First-Price Sealed auction presents a good performance because the auctioneer may start the auction signaling a maximum price and expecting whatever price below the suggested price. However, it may compromise the social welfare of the system by excessively benefiting users.

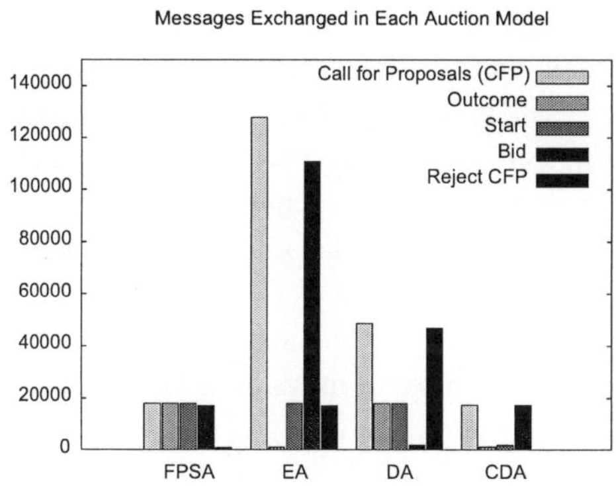

Figure 4. Number of messages exchanged in each auction model.

We have also measured the percentage of budget that users spent in each auction model. Figure 5 (a) presents the amount of budget used in the different auctions. Both English and Dutch auctions present similar performance, while the First-Price sealed allows a user to spend less of her budget. This is due to the bidders being able to choose any price below the one announced. The Continuous double auction generally encourages users to set higher prices as it leads to quick clearance. It is argued that this protocol compensates both bidders and sellers [8]. Therefore, to evaluate whether the Continuous double auction provides better profits to bidders, we measure the percentage of profit made by resource providers. The results shown in Figure 5 (b) demonstrate that

Continuous double auction provides higher profit to providers. In addition, we conclude that First-Price sealed benefits whereas offers the lower profit to providers.

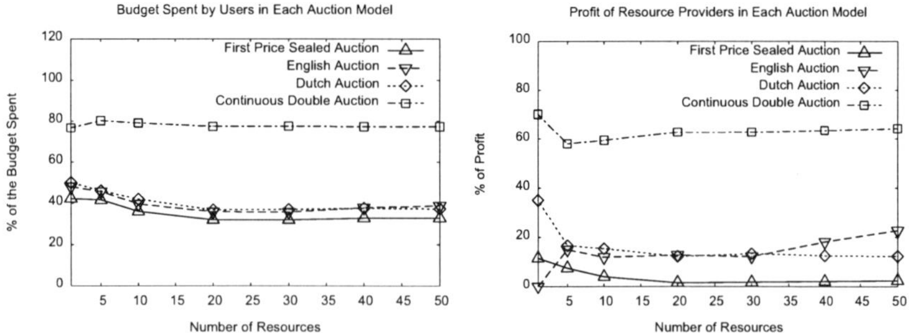

Figure 5. (a) Percentage of aggregated budget spent by users in each auction model. (b) Percentage of aggregated profit made by resource providers.

6. Summary and Conclusion

We presented an investigation on the communication requirements of First-Price sealed, English, Dutch, and Continuous double auctions for resource allocation in Grid computing environments. We have carried out experiments that demonstrate that English auctions present higher communication requirements while Continuous double auctions present least demand of communication. In addition, we demonstrated that English and Dutch auctions lead to the same final prices, even though the number of rounds required might differ.

In addition, we have developed an auction framework that simplifies setting up of performance evaluation experiments in a Grid simulator called GridSim. An example of the use of such framework was presented.

In the future, we plan to improve our experiments by considering the social welfare in the system. In addition, we want to analyze which auction models are better in this regard, which ones benefit providers and which ones benefit consumers and in what scenarios. We also would like to investigate whether it is possible to develop agents that automatically choose one out of a set of auction protocols according to the peculiarities of the Grid environment.

We also plan to carry out further experiments in which auctions are posted in markets and bidders select the auctions in which they are interested. We would like to analyze the communication demand in such scenarios.

Acknowledgments

We thank Anthony Sulistio and Srikumar Venugopal from the University of

Melbourne for their help in extending GridSim and for sharing their thoughts on the topic. We also thank Fernando Koch from Utrecht University for his assistance in improving the quality of this paper.

References

1. I. Foster and C. Kesselman (eds). *The Grid2: Blueprint for a New Computing Infrastructure*. Morgan Kaufmann Publishers Inc., Elsevier, Boston, 2nd edition, 2004.
2. T. Hey and A. E. Trefethen. The UK e-science core programme and the grid. *Future Generation Computer Systems*, 18(8):1017-1031, 2002.
3. L. Paulson. News briefs: Putting a business suit on grid computing. *IEEE Computer*, 38(7):24, July 2005.
4. R.P. McAfee and J. McMillan. Auctions and bidding. *Journal of Economic Literature*, 25(2):699-738, 1987.
5. P. R. Wurman. Dynamic pricing in the virtual marketplace. *IEEE Internet Computing*, 5(2):36-42, March-April 2001.
6. A. Sulistio, G. Poduvaly, R. Buyya, and CK. Tham. Constructing a grid simulation with differentiated network service using gridsim. In *Proceedings of the 6th International Conference on Internet Computing (ICOMP'05)*, Las Vegas, USA, June 2005.
7. R. Buyya, D. Abramson, and S. Venugopal. The Grid Economy. *Special Issue on Grid Computing, Proceedings of the IEEE*, 93(3):698-714, March 2005.
8. D. Grosu and A. Das. Auction-based resource allocation protocols in grids. In *Proceedings of the 16th IASTED International Conference on Parallel and Distributed Computing and Systems*, pages 20-27, Cambridge, MA, USA, November 2004.
9. M. Dalheimer, F. Pfreund, and P. Merz. Agent-based grid scheduling with calana. In *Proceedings of the Second Grid Resource Management Workshop (GRMW 2005)*, Poznan, Poland, 2005.
10. W. Shen, Y. Li, H. H. Ghenniwa, and C. Wang. Adaptive negotiation for agent-based grid computing. In *Proceedings of the Agentcities/AAMAS'02*, pages 32-36, Bologna, Italy, 2002.
11. U. Kant and D. Grosu. Double auction protocols for resource allocation in grids. In *ITCC '05: Proceedings of the International Conference on Information Technology: Coding and Computing (ITCC'05)*, volume I, pages 366-371, Washington, DC, USA, 2005.
12. R. JR. Cassady. *Auctions and Auctioneering*. University of California Press, Berkley and Los Angeles, California, 1967.
13. D. Friedman and J. Rust (eds.). *The double auction market: institutions, theories, and evidence*. Addison-Wesley, 1993.

ADAPTIVE SELF-OPTIMIZING RESOURCE MANAGEMENT FOR THE GRID

CHEN-KHONG THAM & GOKUL PODUVAL

Department of Electrical and Computer Engineering
National University of Singapore
Singapore 117586
E-mail: {eletck,gokul}@nus.edu.sg

Grid computing allows organizations to lower their computing costs by allowing them to share diverse computing resources such as processing power and storage space. These resources can be spread across the world and usage patterns are usually highly dynamic. Hence, Grid resource allocation and management is a challenging problem. In this paper, we propose an adaptive self-optimizing resource management technique to enable: (1) users to select the appropriate Grid resources to enable jobs to meet their quality of service (QoS) requirements, and (2) service providers to allocate the appropriate amount of CPU and network resources to different classes of Grid users. Due to the variable interval between events, the Grid resource management problem is viewed as a Semi-Markov Decision Problem (SMDP) and online reinforcement learning algorithms are proposed. The performance of the proposed algorithms are evaluated in simulation using our enhanced version of the GridSim simulator. The proposed scheme is compatible with pricing and decentralized management schemes for the Grid.

1. Introduction

In grid computing models, users may submit their jobs via brokers to one or many grid processing nodes. These processing nodes may be within the same network domain, or there may be a few network Administrative Domains (AD) away. Hence, resource allocation must also be done at the network domains through which the jobs pass. One way to ensure that jobs meet deadlines is for the user to sign a Service Level Agreement (SLA) with the Grid service provider and all the network domains that his data will pass through. However, this would mean that the location of the Grid processing nodes will need to be fixed and known in advance. This takes away a lot of the flexibility of the Grid since the actual locations of resources being used is supposed to be transparent to the user.

Grid service providers can maximize their resource usage and reduce supervision of their systems by using dynamic resource management mechanisms. In this paper, we propose reinforcement learning (RL) (also known as neuro-dynamic programming (NDP))-based mechanisms that can observe the load and other conditions at a resource and learn resource allocation policies without the need for external supervision. The advantage of using RL is that it does not require careful configuration or offline training before being used in practice. Grid and network administrators can deploy RL-based agents on their network and computation nodes, and expect them to learn and implement the optimal policy over a period of time. Another advantage is that RL techniques do not stop learning and continually adapts to changing conditions in the Grid and network such as changing resource demand patterns or characteristics of resources. This reduces the need for administrators to continuously monitor their resources for unexpected changes.

RL has been used by other researchers to control network bandwidth and CPU allocation. Reference [1] shows how RL can be used to control Per Hop Behavior (PHB) and bandwidth allocation in DiffServ networks with different pricing for different services. Reference [2] studies how specific QoS criteria can be met using a RL-based adaptive packet marking scheme. In the context of the Grid, references [3] and [4] study the problem of resource allocation of computational resources using RL.

We propose an adaptive self-optimizing resource management technique to enable: (1) users to select the appropriate Grid resources to enable jobs to meet their quality of service (QoS) requirements, and (2) service providers to allocate the appropriate amount of CPU and network resources to different classes of Grid users. The unique contribution of this paper is that the Grid resource management problem is viewed as a Semi-Markov Decision Problem (SMDP) and the variable intervals between events in the Grid are taken into account, thus leading to greater analytical correctness and improved performance. In addition, both computational and networking resources are taken into consideration, unlike most works which only consider one or the other.

2. Markov Decision Process (MDP) and Reinforcement Learning

Markov Decision Process (MDP) is a powerful and general mathematical framework for modeling the behavior of systems with states which evolve over time in response to actions taken. RL/NDP techniques can be used to solve an MDP in an online manner and determine a *policy* which specifies the appropriate actions in different situations or *states* to maximize a numerical reward signal over a period of time. Comprehensive treatments on MDP and RL can be found in [5] and [6]. An MDP problem becomes a Semi-Markov Decision Process (SMDP) problem when the service or sojourn times between actions are not fixed but are drawn from a general probability distribution.

In our problem of Grid resource management, we applied two reinforcement learning algorithms: (1) Watkins Q(λ) [7], and (2) Semi-Markovian Average Reward Technique (SMART) [8].

2.1. *Watkins Q(λ)*

Watkins Q(λ) [7] is an off-policy Temporal Difference (TD) learning method. It combines one-step Q-learning with eligibility traces. In one step Q-Learning, the agent uses the following update rule:

$$Q(s_t, a_t) \leftarrow Q(s_t, a_t) + \alpha[R_{t+1} + \gamma max_a Q(s_{t+1}, a) - Q(s_t, a_t)] \qquad (1)$$

The $Q^{\pi}(s, a)$ function is the perceived value of taking action a at state s under policy π. If the agent follows policy π and maintains an separate average for actions from each state, the average will converge to the Q-value for that state. Equation 1 above is known as one-step Q-learning because the Q-value of a state-action pair is only updated with the Q-value of the next state-action pair visited. The term $[R_{t+1} + \gamma max_a Q(s_{t+1}, a) - Q(s_t, a_t)]$ in equation 1 is known as the *Temporal Difference* (TD) error. A positive TD error indicates that the tendency to select action a_t at state s_t should be increased and vice-versa.

According to Watkins Q(λ), equations 2 and 3 below are used to update the Q-values for state-action pairs. Whenever an exploratory action is taken instead of a greedy one, all the trace values are set to 0. The RL agent calculates the TD errors according to equation 2, and updates a function approximator storing the Q-values according to equation 3.

$$\delta \leftarrow R + \gamma \max_a Q(s_{t+1}, a) - Q(s_t, a_t) \qquad (2)$$

$$Q(s_t, a_t) \leftarrow Q(s_t, a_t) + \alpha \delta e(s_t, a) \qquad (3)$$

2.2. *SMART*

SMART [8] is an RL technique to solve Semi-Markov Decision Process (SMDP) problems. The Bellman optimality equation for SMDPs can be stated as follows: there exists a scalar χ^* and a value function V^* satisfying the system of equations

$$V^*(s,a) = R(s,a) - \chi^* \tau(s,a) + \sum_{s' \in \mathbb{S}} P_{ss'}(a) \max_{a' \in \mathbb{A}_{s'}} V^*(s',a), \forall s \in \mathbb{S} \tag{4}$$

where $\tau(s,a)$ is the average sojourn time of the SMDP in state s under action a.

Jobs in the Grid take variable amounts of time to complete. This time not only depends on the number of Grid jobs, but it will also change according to the local load at the grid node. Since the sojourn times are not fixed, the problem can be appropriately modeled as an SMDP.

The term $V(s,a)$ in equation 4 can be calculated using SMART in an online manner using equation 5 shown below

$$V_{new}(s,a) = (1-\alpha_m)V_{old}(s,a) + \alpha_m \left(R(s,s',a) - \mathcal{AR}_m \tau(s,s',a) + \max_{a'} V_{old}(s',a') \right) \tag{5}$$

where $V_{new}(s,a)$ is the new calculated value of action a in state s at the mth decision epoch, α is the learning rate at that epoch for updating the value of the state-action pair, $\mathcal{AR}_m$ is the average reward rate, which is updated according to equation 6.

$$\mathcal{AR}_m = (1-\beta_{m-1})\mathcal{AR}_{m-1} + \beta_{m-1} \frac{T(m-1)\mathcal{AR}_{m-1} + R(s',s,a)}{T(m)} \tag{6}$$

T(m) is the total time spent in all visited states until the mth decision period and β_m is a learning rate parameter. The learning rates α_m and β_m, and the exploration rate ϵ_m are decayed slowly to 0.

3. Reinforcement Learning-based Resource Allocation

We consider the Grid usage scenario in which a user sends his job to a local broker. The User Broker (UB), running an RL agent, decides where to submit the job depending on the requirements of the job, availability and load conditions on Grid nodes, budget and time constraints etc. Once the Grid node is chosen, the UB connects to the Grid Resource (GR) and sends the job to it. The data passes through a few routers in one or more ADs before reaching the GR. The GRs and routers also run RL agents within themselves. These agents can change the resource allocation policy where they are running.

Each job has a deadline and a positive or negative reward is generated depending on whether the job is completed within deadline. The reward is sent to the RL agents which use it to update their policies according to the equations shown in the previous section.

Service differentiation allows certain classes of traffic to have better service through higher priority access to system resources than others. Service differentiation on the Grid resource nodes and network routers can be achieved through resource provisioning or reservation. We implemented Self Clocked Fair Queueing (SCFQ) to provide provisioning and Rate-Jitter scheduling to provide reservation on routers. SCFQ is a simple to implement approximation of Weighted Fair Queuing (WFQ). On Grid Resources (GRs), for provisioning, we implemented a scheduler that prioritizes jobs by assigning weights using an algorithm that approximates Generalized Processor Sharing (GPS). To provide reservation services, we implemented a mechanism in which each jobs get assigned a certain share of the CPU cycles, depending on its class. These schemes have been studied in simulation and have also been implemented on an actual Grid testbed. Due to space constraints, only results from the resource reservation case are presented in this paper.

4. Grid Simulation Scenario and Results

In this section, we discuss the Grid and network scenario which we studied in simulation and provide performance results for the RL-based adaptive techniques described above. We used the GridSim [9] grid simulation system which we enhanced with differentiated services and network components [10]. The simulation experiments compare commonly-used static resource allocation methods with the proposed adaptive resource reservation methods.

4.1. *Simulation Scenario*

Figure 1 shows the system topology under consideration. The scenario consists of two Grid users, two Grid Resources (GRs) and two routers between the users and GRs. All the network links have a bandwidth of 1 Megabit per second (Mbps) and a propagation delay of 5 ms. The MTU for each packet in the network is 1,000 bytes. The routers are able to process data at 1 Mbps. GR1 has a processing capacity of 250 Million Instructions

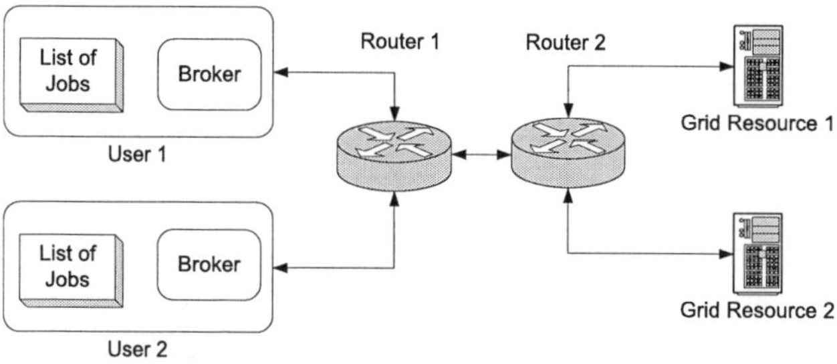

Figure 1. Simulation scenario

Per Second (MIPS), while GR2 has a processing capacity of 350 MIPS.

Table 1. Characteristics of Jobs in Simulation Scenario

Class	Job Size (MIPS)	Data Size (bytes)	Mean Generation Delay(s)	Deadline (s)
1	150	50,000	2.5	4
2	300	100,000	2.5	15

Table 1 shows the characteristics of the two classes of jobs that were sent to the GRs through the routers. Class 2 jobs require more processing power and network bandwidth, whereas Class 1 jobs require a lower response time, i.e. Class 2 jobs model bulk or background jobs, whereas Class 1 jobs model jobs which require immediate attention and fast response times. User 1 always sends Class 1 jobs, while User 2 sends Class 2 jobs. The delay between sending out two jobs is determined by an exponential distribution. Each simulation is run for 25,000 seconds of simulation time.

4.2. *Simulation Experiments*

Four simulation experiments were carried out to investigate the performance of the different resource reservation schemes:

- RR: The UBs run in Round Robin (RR) mode in which jobs are sent alternatively to GR1 and GR2. GRs and routers use static reservation with a fixed amount of resources allocated for each class: CPU cycles at GR1 is shared 1:1 among Class 1 and 2, GR2 reserves 65% of its bandwidth for Class 1, and the rest is reserved for Class 2.

- ExpAvg: The UBs maintain an exponentially weighted average of the job response time of each GR according to

$$EA_{it} = \alpha * \rho_{it} + (1 - \alpha) * EA_{i(t-1)}$$

where EA_{it} is the exponentially weighted average of resource i at time t, ρ_{it} is the response time of the last job at resource i and α is the learning rate, which is set to $\alpha = 0.5$. A new job is always sent to the resource with lower average response time. GRs and routers use static reservation, as explained above.
- QL: The RL agents at the UBs, routers and GRs use the Watkins Q(λ) algorithm to learn the reservation policy.
- SMART: The RL agents at the UBs, routers and GRs use the SMART algorithm to learn the reservation policy.

4.3. *RL agent configuration*

The following applies to both the Q(λ) and SMART RL agents.
State Space - At the UBs, the state is the response time of the job. The response time of a resource is a good indicator of its load, since higher response times indicate a high load on the system. Since each UB sends only one class of job, the state for the UB is only the response times of jobs of that class experienced at each GR, i.e.

$$s_{UB} = \{\rho_{GR1}, \rho_{GR2}\}$$

where ρ_{GR1} is the response time of GR1 and ρ_{GR2} is the response time of GR2. Figure 2 shows the timeline of job generation and completion for class k jobs. The current state of the system is always determined by the response time of the last job that was completed. For example, at time $t = 14$, the state dimension for that class is $\{\rho_{14,k}\} = \{7\}$, where as at time $t = 18$, the state dimension for that class is $\{\rho_{18,k}\} = \{15\}$.

In the case of RL agents at routers and GRs, the state is the service levels being provided to each class of job. Since we have two classes of jobs, the state s_t at time t is

$$s_t = \phi_{1,t}, \phi_{2,t}$$

where $\phi_{i,t}$ is the service level for class 1 at time t and $\phi_{2,t}$ is the service level for class 2. In the case of resource reservation, the service levels are determined by the bandwidth share for routers and CPU share for GRs.
Action Space: At routers, bandwidth reservation is provided by using a rate-jitter scheduler. The RL agents choose a reservation level pair from

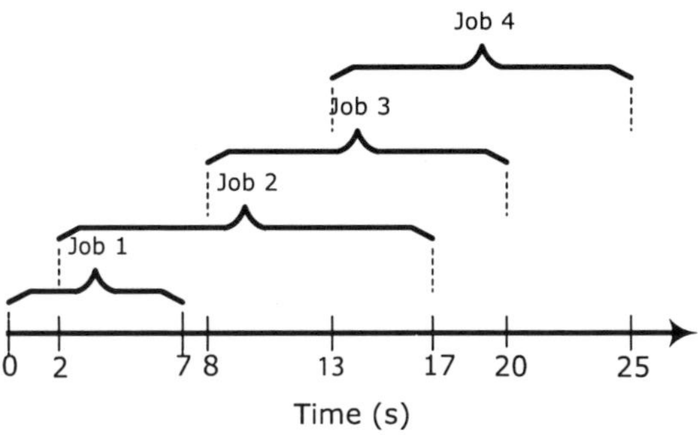

Figure 2. Timeline showing generation and completion of jobs

following list: {(40%,60%), (50%,50%), (60%,40%), (70%,30%)}, where the first element of the set represents the percentage of CPU cycles reserved for Class 1, and the second element represents the percentage of CPU cycles reserved for Class 2.

At GRs, RL agents choose the reservation levels to use for each class of job. Similar to the routers, the reservation levels that the agent can choose are as follows: {(40%,60%), (50%,50%), (60%,40%), (70%,30%)}. The CPU cycles reserved for a class of jobs is shared equally among all jobs of that class running simultaneously on that GR.

4.4. *Results*

Table 2 shows the average response time, which is the total time taken to submit, execute and get results from a job, for the two classes, while Table 3 shows the average processing time, which is the time spent by jobs at the GRs. It can be seen that the response times for Class 1 and 2 are significantly better when the agents at UBs, routers and GRs use the Q(λ) or SMART algorithm, compared to the RR or ExpAvg cases. The performance of the SMART scheme is noticeably better than Q(λ) as it is better able to capture the system dynamics when there is a variable interval between events.

Table 2. Average Response Time of Jobs

Class	RR (s)	ExpAvg (s)	QL (s)	SMART (s)
1	2.677932	2.614117	2.064217	2.016163
2	5.630762	21.276755	4.651910	4.423825

Table 3. Average Processing Time of Jobs

Class	RR (s)	ExpAvg (s)	QL (s)	SMART (s)
1	0.962621	0.880351	0.307630	0.257287
2	2.815509	18.158761	1.742260	1.550361

In the case of RR, the resource managers are unable to select the appropriate resources to match the requirements of user applications, while in the case of ExpAvg, the lack of a predictive ability causes the resource manager to switch resources only when delays are high, which is too late and may cause oscillatory behavior, thus leading to high response and processing times.

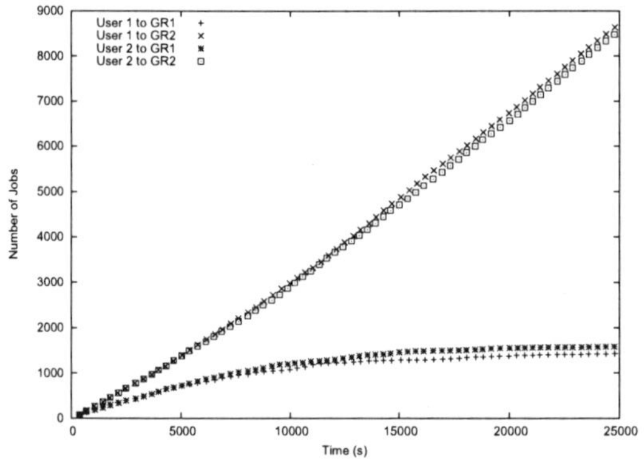

Figure 3. Distribution of jobs at different GRs

Figure 3 shows how the number of jobs of each class which are sent to the different GRs change over time when UBs use Q(λ) to learn the job scheduling policy. Initially, both GR1 and GR2 receive an equal share of Class 1 and Class 2 jobs. Due to its lower processing capacity, GR1 becomes congested and the response time increases significantly. The RL agents adapt, and subsequently, both UB1 and UB2 send fewer jobs to GR1.

5. Conclusion

From the earlier sections of this paper, we can see the usefulness of adopting an MDP/SMDP formulation of the Grid resource management problem and the effectiveness of the Q(λ) and SMART online RL algorithms to select and allocate resources in computational and network nodes in the presence of dynamic traffic patterns and different resource capacities. The effectiveness of this approach with a static pricing plan had been described in [1]. Our next step is to extend the formulation and technique to the dynamic resource pricing situation [11, 12] in which resource managers set prices depending on a variety of factors and users select resources to meet QoS requirements and budget constraints.

References

1. T.C.K. Hui and C.K. Tham, *Adaptive Provisioning of Differentiated Services Networks based on Reinforcement Learning*, IEEE Transactions on Systems, Man & Cybernetics, Vol. 33, No. 4, IEEE, Nov 2003, pp. 492–501
2. C.K. Tham and Y. Liu, *Assured end-to-end QoS through adaptive marking in multi-domain differentiated services networks* Computer Communications, Special Issue on Current Areas of Interest in End-to-End QoS, Vol. 28, Issue 18, Nov. 2005, Elsevier, pp 2009–2019
3. D. Vengerov, *A Reinforcement Learning Framework for Utility-Based Scheduling in Resource-Constrained Systems*, Technical Report SMIL TR-2005-141, Sun Microsystems Laboratories, 2005
4. A. Galstyan,K. Czajkowski and K. Lerman, *Resource Allocation in the Grid Using Reinforcement Learning*, International Conference on Autonomous Agents and Multiagent Systems, Columbia University, New York City, USA, 19–23 July 2004
5. R.S. Sutton and A.G. Barto, *Reinforcement Learning: An Introduction*, MIT Press, Cambridge, MA, USA, 1998
6. L.P. Kaelbling, M.L. Littman and A.P. Moore, *Reinforcement Learning: A Survey*, Journal of Artificial Intelligence Research, vol 4., pp 247–285, 1996
7. C. Watkins *Learning from Delayed Rewards*, PhD. thesis, King's College, Cambridge, United Kingdom, 1989
8. T.K. Das, A. Gosavi, S. Mahadevan and N. Marchalleck, *Solving Semi-Markov Decision Problems Using Average Reward Reinforcement Learning*, Management Science, vol. 45, no. 4, pp 560–574, USA, 1999
9. R. Buyya and M. Murshed, *GridSim: A Toolkit for the Modeling and Simulation of Distributed Resource Management and Scheduling for Grid Computing*, The Journal of Concurrency and Computation: Practice and Experience (CCPE), Wiley Press, May 2002
10. A. Sulistio, G. Poduval, R. Buyya and C.K. Tham, *Constructing A Grid Simulation with Differentiated Network Service Using GridSim*, Proceedings of 2005 International Conference on Internet Computing (ICOMP'05), 2005
11. A. Dogan and F. Özgüner, *Scheduling Independent Tasks with QoS Requirements in Grid Computing with Time-Varying Resource Prices*, GRID 2002, pp 58–69
12. G. Tesauro and J. Kephart, *Pricing in agent economies using multi-agent Q-learning*, Fifth European Conference on Symbolic and Quantitative Approaches to Reasoning with Uncertainty, July 1999.

Market Managed Operation of the Internet

INFORMATION-RESOURCE ECONOMICS — THE INTERSECTION BETWEEN GRID ECONOMICS AND INFORMATION ECONOMICS

DR. CHRIS KENYON
DEPFA BANK PLC[*] DUBLIN, IRELAND
email: Chris.Kenyon@yahoo.com

Grid Economics looks at the economics of resources such as computational capacity, storage capacity and network capacity. That is, the economics of non-storable resources. In contrast, Information Economics looks at information as it exists in, for examples, CD's or DVD's, which have very low marginal costs of production. Here, I will examine the intersection between Grid and Information Economics which I will label Information-Resource Economics, focussing first on defining and clarifying the concept of Information-Resources. Information-Resources can be print books whose pages are made available, for a price, via the web. Alternatively a resource can be a blog, or special interest site, that produces revenue via advertisements. Alternatively an information-resource can be an individual song track. A specific characteristic of these information-resources is that their value comes partly from their content and party how they are accessible. Their content — at a single point in time — may have low marginal cost of production but their value comes from accessibility etc. (e.g. reputation for a blog). Thus we consider both the value of the resources for their owners and the total cost of different types of ownership of these resources. We examine cases of successful creation of information-resources and draw conclusions both for information-resources in general and for Grid resources in particular.

1. Introduction

Grid Economics deals with the value and monetization of coordinated resource sharing [RWT00,Buy02,RBV05,GCB05]. Information Economics likewise deals with the value and monetization of content [MMV94,Me97,SV99,Odl01]. Here we look at the intersection of the two in the context of the Internet that we label Information-Resource Economics. This is a fast growing area of practical interest to companies such as Amazon, Apple, eBay, Google, Microsoft, and Yahoo. This paper will attempt to define and describe

[*]affiliation at date of conference, see acknowledgements for more details.

Information-Resource Economics in a way that leads to further understanding of its commercial potential and use. Note that this work is partially anticipated by [Var06] looking at the value of a position on a web-page. The particular characteristics of Information-Resources are the mixing of information and resource attributes and their monetization. Because of the -resource aspect of information resources they depend directly on their value chain and life-cycle of use. This also leads to many possibilities for their monetization which we will explore. We will also consider the infrastructure requirements to support Information-Resources and their implications for Grid resources in general.

Previous work has highlighted the role of discrimination in price setting [SV99] for information goods. Here we incorporate the resource aspect to focus on information-resources and their valuation. Information-resouces are essentially mixes of the two concepts: of resources (the capacity for action or service), and information (or content). Thus we can view a blog as content that is discriminated[a] by its location, and *by its dynamic nature.* It is also easy to prevent direct copying for two reasons: firstly the search engine that ranks the blog highly will also make copies obvious; and secondly the blog is dynamic.

This paper is organized as follows. We start with definitions. Then we consider a set of real-world examples and apply the definitions to illustrate their utility in bringing out the possibilities for monetization in Information-Resources. We next look at infrastructure requirements to support Information-Resources. Finally we draw conclusions both for Information-Resources in general and for Grid Economics in particular.

2. Definitions

- Monetization: the creation of a value stream in dollars/euros/etc from information, resources, information-resources, etc.
- Information: any type of content, e.g. written notes, printed book, digital music recording, offer-for-sale, etc.
- Resource: and type of capacity to perform or support a service, e.g. computational power, bandwidth, web-site location, geographical location, temporal location.
- Information-Resource: items with the characteristics of both information and resources. E.g. a web-site — this has both location and

[a]We use discrimination to mean any attribute that information resources, or their consumers, can be segmented on.

content. The location is both absolute in the sense of a URL, and relative in the sense of all the web-sites that link to it or contain related information. It is also dynamic in the sense of its ranking on search engines relative to different keyword searches.

- Object: generic term for information, resources, and information-resources.
- Monetized object: an object generating an income stream.
- Grid Economics: the economics of resource sharing in the context of intra-nets and/or the Internet.
- Information Economics: the economics of information.
- Internet Information-Resource Economics: the economics of information-resources in the context of intra-nets and/or the Internet.

3. Information-Resources

We start with a series of examples of actual and potential information resources. Following these examples will we summarize their characteristics and maturity.

3.1. *Examples*

3.1.1. *Search Engine*

A search engine is basically a meta-site whose information content is either largely (Yahoo) or completely (Google) determined by (and relative to) the user, not by the site creator. In this sense they are the perfect advertising platform in that the user creates the pages that the user views. However, without additional information, e.g. credit card history and bank records for the user (etc) this view of the user is necessarily incomplete.

Search engines are absolute locations offering search. Their resource is the screen area not devoted to search results.

Monetization is by subletting, and different classes of advertising. This is a mature market for the very incomplete user view that is currently taken. Without knowing how a user actually spends money the difference between views, clicks, and purchases is necessarily highly uncertain.

3.1.2. *Web-Site*

A web-site can contain information, e.g. a site on a specialist subject, or can be a set of pointers to other (types of) information (e.g. downloads).

A web-site is a virtual location. The resource a web-site represents is, for example, its location on a set of search-engine results for a given keyword. That is, the resource aspect of a web-site is defined relative to other web-sites, keyword-search frequency distributions, and ranking engines. Virtual location values are similar to physical location values (e.g. close to main street and with good links to the airport) except that the timescale for changes, in the determinants of the value of the location, is much shorter in the virtual world. For example, its much faster to add new links from a web-site than to build a new road. A few web-sites are sufficiently well known to be virtual locations in and of themselves (e.g. www.amazon.com, www.ebay.com, www.google.com, www.yahoo.com).

A web-site can be monetized either by sales of things (e.g. books on a retail site like amazon.com) or by sales of itself (e.g. advertising or subletting). The second method is especially common on search engines whose virtual space for advertising is unlimited with respect to different search terms although highly limited in terms of screen real-estate (most users will look at only a few pages of results). Subletting has become common via programs such as Google's AdSense where a site permits another (legal) entity to choose which adverts will be placed on it.

The themes we have outlined above for web-sites are repeated and specialized in different ways for most of our other examples. The interest lies in exactly how these themes are adapted to different niches. Current search capabilities are making the monetization of more and more niches viable via the long-tail argument[b] [And04]. This states that rare events occur commonly in large enough systems. I.e. even highly specialist sites can be monetized provided their customers can find them easily.

One theme not highly developed for a generic web-site is total cost of ownership or use. This will be explored below in the context of song downloads and ring-tone downloads.

3.1.3. *Retail Web-Sites*

We use Amazon as our example here because it has some of the best developed user tracking and community features of mainstream retail sites.

Amazon is a virtual, but well known location. In common with search engines Amazon page contents (information) is largely determined by the user's actions. Hence it is a very adapted sales and advertising platform.

[b] http://www.thelongtail.com/the_long_tail/

The resource available is the page area not used for search results. Amazon has rudimentary user communities, e.g. user-lists. However, there are few, if any, explicit links to social networks which would appear natural given the extent of book clubs etc.

3.1.4. *Blogs*

Blogs are specialized web-sites for personal experiences (with one or many contributors) or (more generally) amateur journalism on specific topics, generally hobbies, products, or companies. Currently many companies have set up their own blogs and bloggers are employed full time in a small number of cases. Information on an active blog is dynamic with entries added on a timescale of days.

The resource a blog represents, like a web-site, is a virtual location on search engine listings relative to keywords, web-site links, and identities (i.e. the reputations of the people blogging on the site).

Blogs are monetized by direct payments to the author, when employed by a company, or by advertising or subletting.

3.1.5. *Print books and handwritten notes*

Print books and handwritten notes are becoming accessible from the Internet, e.g. via Amazon's search inside the book feature, Google Print, and Google's research effort with several universities for searching handwriting. The information they contain is their content, relative to searches, relative to the state-of-the-art for textbooks, and relative to currency for new releases etc.

The resource that they represent is their use for leisure or business. For example, most people prefer to read books on paper rather than on a screen. Users of a textbook may only require a particular chapter or formula, potentially this can be used from a screen.

These resources are monetized by sales of themselves and represent a half-way stage to song-downloads and ringtone-downloads that we cover next.

3.1.6. *Song-downloads and ringtone-downloads*

Song-downloads and ringtone-downloads cannot be considered in isolation: it makes no sense to consider a ringtone without considering mobile phones. For a few years (i.e. Napster's early peak) it was possible to consider song-downloads without considering the player, but even then the download system (i.e. PC + internet connection + connection subscription) needed to be included.

The resource here is the download-and-play system. E.g. Apple's iTunes software on a PC and, optionally, an iPod player (now in generation 4 or 5 with the iPod Nano).

Songs and ringtones can be monetized in two distinct ways: sales or subscriptions, and litigation. Litigation is a very inefficient direct method of monetization, e.g. via court proceedings against file-sharers, because there are (anecdotally) many file-sharers and the income stream generated is irregular. However, by making people include potential legal and reputational costs into their total cost of ownership litigation has changed the download/fileshare landscape (e.g. Napster has now transformed into a legal service). Monetization via direct sales is a more reliable, e.g. Apple's iTunes sold its one billionth song recently.

With sings and ringtones the total cost of ownership (TCO) is highly important. As mentioned this includes potential legal costs for illegal activities (when present). However, a more important factor is convenience. How easy is it to listen to the songs? Is it easy to understand the pricing structure? Is it easy to understand the download service contract? For example, can the songs be burnt to CD for longer term storage (N.B. retail hard disk warranties range from one to three years at best)? Can the songs bee transferred between computers easily? For this category of information-resource consumer TCO is an important determination of monetization success.

3.1.7. *Hard disk drives, personal and corporate*

Hard disk drives are becoming information-resources. Clearly hard disks have always been physical locations but with the advent of desktop search linked to the internet (e.g. Google Desktop, MSN Search, Yahoo Desktop Search, etc.) it has become possible to monetize them.

Logical extensions of hard disks for functions, e.g. email stores on servers, is a route that was first turned into an information resource by Gmail enabling monetization of personal information. However, payment to users has — so far — been in kind, i.e. use of the system. The actual cash-stream has gone to the intermediary (Google).

Monetization of corporate disk drives, as opposed to consumer disk drives, is hardly developed as yet.

3.1.8. *Credit cards*

Credit cards are the most un-exploited information-resource to date. This information details exactly what individuals actually buy so is highly valuable in terms of advertising. The resource could be constructed as a website with (secure) access to the spiders of choice to the individual or credit card company. There are clearly privacy issues to be addressed but these can certainly be resolved because modern cryptographic/privacy protocols allow selective revelation of information. In fact in the extreme case of zero-knowledge proofs it is possible to prove that information is known without revealing it. Thus we would anticipate significant developments in resource creations and monetization of credit card information in the near future.

3.1.9. *Magazine subscriptions and social-networking-software*

Further under-exploited information-resources are magazine subscriptions, and all membership and subscriptions in general, including social networking software memberships. As with credit card data the information content of these in undeniable. These also require transformation into resources by bringing them in to the general access paradigm of the Internet or similar. By similar we mean any linking method which permit network externalities to be effective.

3.1.10. *Physical locations*

The information present at physical locations is currently very poorly developed. This will require more widespread use of location sensitive personal devices (either PDA's or cell phones) and appropriate understanding of consumer choice. Few people want to see every possible advertisement continuously from all stores within, say, 10 minutes travel time.

The resource in question is relative to the location itself (e.g. an airport) and relative to other locations, e.g. restaurants or gas stations within 10 minutes travel time.

Monetization via location-linked advertising (e.g. of nearby restaurants) and sales (e.g. of cinema tickets) is only seen in a handful of examples outside PC's. For example some vending machines can be accessed via cell phone. PC's themselves are poor platforms for location based advertising (e.g. as supported by Google Earth) because PC's are not mobile devices unlike cell phones.

3.1.11. *Functional locations*

Functional locations are locations associated with functions, e.g. gas stations or supermarkets. These are information-resources par excellence. They contain large amounts of information from a combination of location, contents, function, and time (e.g. of day). They are also resources, again for the same set of factors.

Functional locations are mostly monetized by sales of things, e.g. petrol/gas and conventional subletting of physical locations (e.g. all the small outlets in a supermarket). However virtual subletting is becoming common via advertisements on monitors. These are starting to be time-of-day sensitive, with, presumably, prices to match. However, the link to identity or some derivative of identity (e.g. single shopper, shopper with children) is not yet developed.

3.2. *Summary: Characteristics and Maturity*

description	information	resource	monetization and maturity
search engine	search results	results pages	advertising, mature
web-site	local content, links	search engine ranking	sales, advertising, mature
blog	experiences, links	search engine ranking	advertising, mature
books	local content	physical, search engine ranking	sales, advertising, developing
song-, ringtone-downloads	sound	download system	sales, limited advertising, developing
hard-disk drives	local content	personal computer	none as yet, hinted at with Gdrive[Goo06c]
magazine subscriptions	magazine, subscribers	pages	mostly conventional advertising
physical locations	very limited, undeveloped	location	very limited = unexploited
functional locations	limited, undeveloped	location+activity	limited = unexploited

We summarize by categories: information; resource; monetization and maturity. Maturity of information-resources is generally related to their monetization. Indeed, monetization can be taken as a direct measure of their maturity.

We have largely excluded mass media such as TV, radio, and newspapers because of our Internet-centric focus. These mass media are already monetized and mature as far as mass audiences are concerned. However, with the advent of personal video recorders (PVRs) such as TiVo, podcasts, and podcast radio, a new era in personalized advertising has become possible but is totally immature at present.

4. Infrastructure Requirements

The common denominator of current commercially successful information-resources is their ease of use and focus on the customer. This is true both for price setting (e.g. the auctions of Google Ad Words) for commercial users, and for cases where flat pricing prevails (e.g. iTunes) thus removing one barrier to retail acceptance.

Successful infrastructures make themselves effectively invisible so that the service or content become dominant. If we compare typical successful information-resource infrastructures (e.g. eBay, iTunes, Amazon, Google search) to typical Grid infrastructures we can observe two distinct categories. Firstly there are the proprietary Grids supported by vendors (e.g. Platform Computing, Data Synapse) or internal IT departments. This type of grid is present in a large proportion of top banks today and is in routine use. Here there is clear focus on the customer and on users. The second category is more the compute-power-available type that is typified by IBM's Deep Computing or Sun's cpu's on demand offering (not to be confused with Sun's N1 grid software). This more component-type focus leaves much of the work to the user.

Grid markets, that is, markets for accessible cpu power, are quite undeveloped although they have been regularly proposed from the mainframe era [Sut68] onwards [WHH+92,RN98,RWT00] sometimes with a set of caveats [GCB05]. The problem here appears to be their general purpose nature, which makes customer focus difficult. In the context of this paper we might suggest that resources without information have a difficult time developing a business model. However, the widespread deployment of service oriented architectures (SOA)[d] could decouple the information requirement from the resource

[d]http://www.service-architecture.com/web-services/articles/

requirement and thus enable successful Grid markets.

5. Conclusions

WThe objective of this paper is to introduce Information-Resources as the subject of the intersection between the previous fields of Grid Economics and Information Economics which we call Information-Resource Economics. Through the examples of information-resources given we have demonstrated their commercial success and suggest that this is precisely because of their combined attributes. Information alone can be either unusable (MP3 tracks still require players) or too costly to users without the appropriate resources (the download and player system for song-downloads). In this sense we broaden the focus with information-resources beyond pricing content to consider total cost of ownership. With this focus it becomes simpler to understand how monetization can spread to many on and off-line niches that are currently either undeveloped (e.g. credit card data) or very incompletely developed (hard disk drives).

Privacy concerns abound with spreading information-resource monetization, and form a suitable topic for further developments in the cryptography/privacy space. One striking possibility is the applicability of zero-knowledge proofs[FS87,BDMP91]. These could potentially enable advertising to specific individuals without the individuals having to reveal significant personal data, just having to prove that they belonged to advertiser-interesting categories.

The implications for Grid markets are less immediately positive; commercial success in our examples seems to require both information and resources. This also points out that perhaps Grid markets should specialize and thus incorporate information (e.g. rendering applications) specific to chosen user segments (e.g. audio-visual digital media). Alternatively the widespread deployment of service oriented architectures (SOA) could decouple the information requirement from the resource requirement and thus enable successful Grid markets.

Acknowledgements

The author gratefully acknowledges useful discussions with Giorgos Cheliotis and Steven Miller. Much of this thinking was developed whilst at IBM

service-oriented_architecture_soa_definition.html

Research but only came into focus with the GECON organizers' generous invitation.

References

And04. C. Anderson. The long tail. Wired Magazine, 12(10), 2004.

BDMP91. Manuel Blum, Alfredo De Santis, Silvio Micali, and Guiseppe Persiano. Non-interactive zero-knowledge. *SIAM Journal of Computing*, 20(6):1084–1118, 1991.

Buy02. R. Buyya. *Economic-based Distributed Resource Management and Scheduling for Grid Computing.* PhD Thesis, Monash University, Melbourne, Australia, 2002.

FS87. Amos Fiat and Adi Shamir. How to prove yourself: Practical solutions to identification and signature problems. In Andrew M. Odlyzko, editor, *Advances in Cryptology — CRYPTO '86*, volume 263, pages 186–194. Springer Verlag, 1987.

GCB05. C. Kenyon G. Cheliotist and R. Buyya. 10 lessons from finance for commercial sharing of it resources. *Peer-to-Peer Computing: The Evolution of a Disruptive Technology*, Idea Group Publishing:244–264, 2005.

Goo06. Google. Google analyst day. http://investor.google.com/pdf/20060302_analyst_day.pdf, 2006.

Me97. L. McKnight and J. Bailey (editors). *Internet Economics.* MIT Press, 1997.

MMV94. J. MacKie-Mason and H. Varian. *Public Access to the Internet (eds B. Kahin and J. Keller*, chapter Pricing the Internet. Prentice-Hall, 1994.

Odl01. A. Odlyzko. Internet pricing and the history of communications. *Computer Networks*, 36:493–517, 2001.

RBV05. D. Abranson R. Buyya and S. Venugopal. The grid economy. *Proceedings of the IEEE*, 93:698–714, 2005.

RN98. O. Regev and N. Nisan. The popcorn market online markets for computational resources. *First International Conference On Information and Computation Economies*, 1998.

RWT00. J. Brevik R. Wolski, J.S. Plank and T.Bryan. G-commerce: Market formulations controlling resource allocation on the computational grid. *University of Tennessee Technical Report*, UT-CS-00-450, 2000.

Sut68. I.E. Sutherland. A futures market in computer time. *Communications of the ACM*, 11, 1968.

SV99. C. Shapiro and H.R. Varian. *Information Rules.* Harvard Business School Press, 1999.

Var06. H. Varian. Position auctions. Preprint, 2006.

WHH+92. C. Waldspurger, T. Hogg, B. Huberman, J. Kephart, and S. Stornetta. Spawn: A distributed computational economy. IEEE Transactions on Software Engineering, 1992.

Grid Systems' Economy & Its Operation & Deployment

CHALLENGES IN DESIGNING GRID MARKETPLACES

RAMAYYA KRISHNAN

Heinz School, Carnegie Mellon University
Pittsburgh, PA 15213, USA

KARTIK HOSANAGAR[†]

Operations and Information Management, Wharton School,
University of Pennsylvania
Philadelphia, PA 19104, USA

Grid computing – the shared use of a set of loosely coupled and distributed IT resources across organizations and/or geographies – has made significant headway in recent years. Economic mechanisms ranging from posted prices to auction-based schemes have been proposed to meet the needs of grid resource allocation and scheduling. We do not propose yet another grid economic mechanism in this paper. Instead, we discuss two issues that we believe are fundamental to the economic functioning of the grid – irrespective of the particular mechanism chosen.

The first problem we address is from the perspective of grid resource suppliers and pertains to capacity planning. The grid computing literature has assumed that excess capaçity (of CPU, bandwidth, storage and software licenses) on the grid will exist to meet demand from other sources. However, given economic mechanisms, capacity planning becomes subject to these very same economic constraints. The interesting question given the distributed nature of the grid is the effect on social welfare of uncoordinated distributed planning for resource provisioning and how it would compare to social welfare under centralized coordinated capacity planning for grid resources. In this paper, we provide an overview of some of these challenges and propose some techniques from Management Science that may be applicable to these problems.

The second problem is from the perspective of grid consumers and pertains to the estimation of grid resources (software license, CPU, memory, disk space) required to execute a job on the grid. These estimates are required by many market mechanism proposals to enable allocation of resources to jobs on the grid. However, in many settings, developing these estimates are difficult and estimates tend to be noisy and highly variable. This raises a number of questions such as a) What are the implications of this type of noisy estimates on the social welfare of

[†] Work supported by Wharton-SMU grant 2005-06.

grid? b) When resource utilization distributions of jobs are heavy tailed, what is the right way to price access to the resources?

1. Introduction

A key trend in computing today is service-oriented computing, which refers to the sourcing of computing resources such as software, storage and computing cycles from third parties (Foster et al 2001). These trends are driven by various distributed computing technologies. One of the key enabling distributed computing technologies is grid computing. Grid computing refers to the sharing of computing resources such as CPU (processing) cycles among a set of distributed computers across organizations and geographies. Formally, a grid is a type of parallel and distributed system that enables the sharing, selection, and aggregation of geographically distributed "autonomous" resources dynamically at runtime depending on their availability, capability, performance, cost, and user preferences.[1] A well known example of a grid computing project is UC Berkeley's SETI@Home screensaver which allowed Barkeley's SETI project to tap into spare computing power available on millions of PCs that had the screensaver installed. Similarly, Intel's NetBatch Grid project allows the firm to process engineering simulation jobs by using spare computing power available in Intel's various offices. Intel estimates that NetBatch has saved the firm $500M over 10 years and increased computer utilization from 35% to 80% over the same period.[2] Grid computing offers great benefits in solving computationally complex problems by harnessing distributed resources in the form of a virtual organization (see Foster et al 2001). Applications range from financial modeling and weather prediction to molecular modeling for biotech applications. With grid computing maturing from the use of freely provided resources such as in SETI@home to the next generation of organizational infrastructure, there has been considerable focus recently on the design of grid marketplaces (for e.g., Buyya 2002).

Several firms including Sun and IBM have expended considerable resources in trying to establish themselves as primary resource providers in grid markets. Sun Microsystems recently launched the Sun Grid where users can submit large jobs and are charged $1 per CPU hour. IBM, which runs three grid centers in the US and one in France, currently charges $0.47 per CPU hour. Vendors such as Oracle have released products such as Oracle 10g for use on grids. While grid

[1] Source: Gridcomputing.com

[2] Source: http://news.zdnet.com/2100-9595_22-523296.html

computing appears to be focused primarily on shared use of compute resources, markets are emerging – in the related field of shared service computing – for a bundle of software and compute cycles. For example, the emergence of Salesforce.com has promoted the use of CRM software as a service. Initiatives by these large firms are making grid marketplaces a reality.

Since grids can be highly distributed and often function without any central planner, it is important to design market mechanisms that can help produce desirable behavior from each independent decision-making entity in a grid. In this paper, we cover some of the key challenges associated with the design of a grid marketplace. Specifically, we will focus on two issues – i) Determining the cost of distributed coordination in capacity planning decisions in grids. ii) Obtaining accurate estimates of resource requirements for submitted jobs. We will provide an overview of these two challenges and discuss prior work in Management Science that is of relevance in addressing these challenges.

The rest of the paper is organized as follows. In Section 2, we review the related literature on grid marketplaces. In Section 3, we discuss each of the aforementioned challenges associated with the design of grid markets. Finally, we conclude in Section 4.

2. Literature Review

A primary area of focus in grid economics is related to resource allocation. This stream of work studies the use of market mechanisms to allocate computing cycles to incoming jobs. For example, Feldman et al (2005) formulate a resource allocation game and study the efficiency and fairness of the Nash equilibria that results. Wellman et al (2001) propose an auction mechanism to allocate distributed resources to users. Regev and Nisan (1998) also propose an auction mechanism to match buyers and sellers. Other work on market-based resource allocation includes those by Wolski et al (2001), Waldspurger et al (1992), Buyya and Vazhkudai (2001) and Buyya (2002). Market-based resource allocation has also been implemented in the Tycoon system (Lai et al 2004).

3. Challenges in Design of Grid Markets

Grid systems are distributed systems with a number of independent actors that coordinate through a market mechanism. It is important to design market mechanisms in a manner that ensures socially desirable and efficient outcomes are achieved. Below, we review two challenges related to the cost of decentralized coordination and incorrect a priori estimates of resource requirements for jobs submitted to grids.

3.1. Capacity Planning and the Cost of Decentralized Coordination

Distributed systems offer a number of advantages, including scalability and network resilience. However, because control is distributed as well, each of the distributed agents acts (semi) autonomously. Relative to centralized coordination, some efficiency is lost because of this lack of control. It is important to measure this cost and explore approaches to reduce high costs of decentralization.

An interesting issue in this context relates to capacity planning that occurs in a grid environment. In prior studies, researchers have studied resource allocation, scheduling and pricing assuming that capacity already exists in the grid and that the investments in capacity are independent of the underlying business/economic model in place. This was probably reasonable in the first generation of grid initiatives where contributing excess resources to the grid was an after thought and not part of the capacity planning process. However, in second generation grid initiatives as is planned with a functioning market, capacity planning will take grid economics explicitly into account. In a truly distributed grid setting, capacity choices are made by strategic independent nodes based on knowledge of job arrival, payments and capacity choices of other nodes. We plan to study capacity choices with decentralized decision-making and contrast that with capacity choices under coordinated central planning. Specifically, we are interested in the difference in social welfare that obtains in a distributed grid environment with coordinated centralized capacity planning versus an environment in which capacity planning is done by autonomous players. This is related to the "cost of anarchy" literature that has examined similar questions in the context of the Internet (Koutsoupias and Papadimitriou, 1999).

Below, we describe the capacity planning problem with an abstraction of an intra-organizational grid such as that in Intel. Consider a simple grid system with just two nodes. Jobs arrive at a node and may be serviced locally at that node or forwarded to the other node if the local node is congested but other node is free. Assume that each job is completely serviced at one node (i.e., we will tentatively ignore workflows wherein jobs are divided into a sequence of subtasks). A payment mechanism is in place so that a node gets compensated when it services jobs forwarded to it. Job arrival follows a stochastic process with known mean and standard deviation (for e.g., a Poisson process). Each node independently determines its own processing capacity based on arrival rate of jobs, cost of capacity and payments for processing grid jobs.

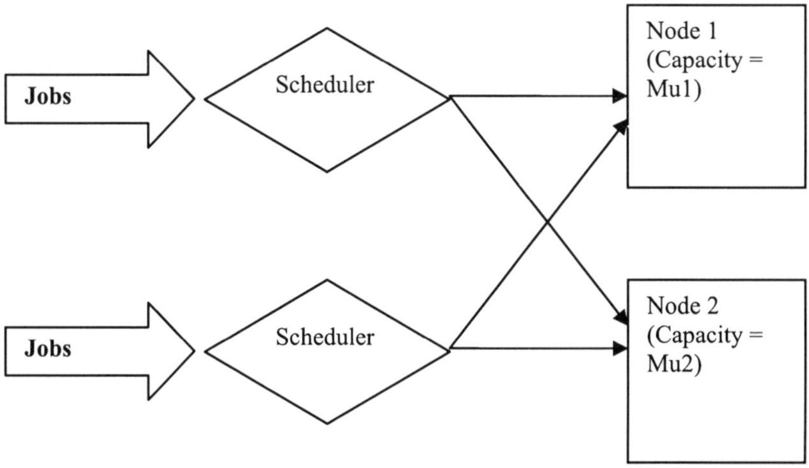

Figure 1. Queuing System for the Two Node Grid

The submitter of the job ultimately cares about the delay in processing the jobs (not just whether the jobs are processed or not). Thus, we assume that the utility is a function of the average delay. The capacity of the two nodes are μ_1 and μ_2 respectively. The cost of capacity is given by $C_1(\mu_1)$ and $C_2(\mu_1)$. In the decentralized case when nodes do not coordinate their capacity decisions, the capacity chosen by node 1 is given by,

$$\max[\lambda_1 U(d(\mu_1)) - C_1(\mu_1)] \tag{1}$$

$d(\mu_1)$ is the expected delay in a queuing system wherein jobs arrive at and are serviced by node 1. U($d(\mu_1)$) is the utility associated with the expected delay. Node 2 solves a similar optimization problem to compute the optimal capacity μ_2. With no coordination among the nodes, efficiency may be lost. However, a central planner can account for the job-arrival process at both nodes and the scheduling algorithm used to forward the jobs to a given node to determine the optimal capacity of the two nodes.

By appropriately modeling the queuing system described in Figure 1, the welfare maximizing optimization problem can be formulated. This will require us to compute $\Pr_1(\mu_1, \mu_1)$, the steady-state probability that a request is forwarded to node 1 given the capacity of the two nodes. Similarly, $d(\mu_1, \mu_2)$, the expected delay in the queuing system will have to be determined. The rich stream of work in queuing including that on multiserver queues is relevant here. These queuing models have been applied to problems of distributed capacity determination in supply chains. Similar models that are formulated keeping the grid context in mind will help shed light on distributed capacity provisioning and the cost of decentralization.

3.2. Estimating Resource Requirements for Jobs

A number of resource scheduling approaches have been proposed in the literature including the Tycoon (Lai et al 2004) and Condor system (Thain et al 2003). Most current systems assume that resource requirements can be estimated a priori by the users. The scheduling systems perform a matchmaking function by matching jobs to resources based on resource requirements and available resources. However, a number of empirical studies have found that users provide highly inaccurate estimates of resources required and job runtime (Mu'alem and Feitelson 2001; Tsafrir et al 2005). These poor estimates continue to be provided by users even when there are strong incentives for truthful reporting. For example, scheduling techniques like backfilling (Mu'alem and Feitelson 2001) schedule the first job in the queue that can be completed given the available resources, thus providing incentives to quote low runtime requirements. Simultaneously, jobs may be killed if the actual runtime is greater than the estimate ensuring that users do not quote low resource and runtime estimates. The inaccuracies in the estimates despite these incentive mechanisms suggest that a fundamental problem is that it is inherently hard for users to estimate resource requirements.

Poor estimates of resource requirements can significantly undermine the efficiency of the scheduling algorithms. Further, job submitters will estimate their costs based on these resource requirement estimates and known pricing policies. Thus, the realized costs may be considerably different from their estimates, causing considerable ex-post regret when costs exceed expectations. This is also not desirable. Solutions are needed to address inefficiencies caused by poor estimates of resource requirements so that buyers can better estimate costs, schedulers can better assign jobs to resources and resource providers can better plan their capacity decisions.

There has been very limited work on addressing these issues. We propose two approaches that researchers and practitioners may adopt to address the problem. The first is to improve the quality of decision support tools provided to job submitters. By analyzing past data on realized completion times of jobs along with job characteristics, it may be possible to better predict the completion time when a new job arrives. A number of machine learning techniques may be applied to learn these prediction rules.

Another interesting approach may be use risk pooling along with an appropriate pricing mechanism. The fundamental idea behind risk pooling is to send heterogeneous jobs to resource providers. Even though there may be considerable variance in resource requirements of individual jobs, the variance in resource requirement of a set of independent jobs would be considerably lower. This follows from the law of large numbers and is a fundamental application of statistical multiplexing. The reduced variation in the pooled jobs allows the provider to better estimate the total resource requirements and hence to plan capacity. Risk pooling has been applied in various domains such as supply procurement and content delivery (Hosanagar et al 2005). The fundamental idea behind risk pooling in Content Delivery Networks (CDN) is that even though there can be considerable variation in demand for individual content provider's content, the variance in the demand for a pooled set of content providers is lower. Thus, a CDN can sign on a large number of heterogeneous content providers as customers. It can then plan capacity based on the pooled demand that has low variance, and can thus lower costs and eliminate the loss of requests. Similarly, risk pooling in a grid setting can be accomplished by the use of a scheduling policy that sends a diverse set of jobs to a resource. This in turn can improve capacity planning by providers in a grid.

In order to mitigate the user's risk of highly variable costs, pricing schemes from content delivery domain may also be applied. For example, percentile-based pricing schemes (Hosanagar et al 2004) are employed in content delivery wherein content providers are charged based on the 95th percentile of the demand. This allows the CDN to charge a higher price to content providers with high mean and/or high variance in demand. At the same time, if the demand distribution is known, the 95th percentile and hence the expected price may be easily computed. This is better than charging for the realized demand as the percentile-based price is more predictable and achieves the objectives of the pricing policy. Similarly, grids may be charge users based on the $90^{th}/95^{th}$ percentile of resources consumed. Thus, even though the exact resource requirement of an individual job cannot be estimated a priori, the 95th percentile for a set of jobs can be predicted when the overall distribution is known. The distribution can be calibrated from the realized resource requirements of past jobs. As a consequence, prices are predictable and stable, thus eliminating user regret from variable bills.

4. Conclusions

The design of grid marketplaces poses challenges, such as the cost of decentralization and the intrinsic difficulty of estimating resource requirements for jobs. Although these issues are unique in many ways, the study of these challenges can benefit from work in Management Science. This includes work on capacity provisioning in supply chains, queuing systems, capacity provisioning and pricing in content delivery, and mechanism design among others. Collaboration between researchers from the two areas holds much promise.

References

1. R. Buyya, Economic-based Distributed Resource Managment and Scheduling for Grid Computing, PhD Thesis, Monash University, Melbourne, Australia, 2002.
2. R. Buyya and S. Vazhkudai, Compute Power Market: Towards a Market-Oriented Grid, The First IEEE/ACM International Symposium on Cluster Computing and the Grid, 2001.
3. M. Feldman, K. Lai and L. Zhang, A price anticipating resource allocation mechanism for distributed shared clusters, Proc. of the 6th ACM conference on Electronic commerce. ACM press, pp 127-136, 2005.
4. I. Foster, C. Kesselman, S. Tuecke, The Anatomy of the Grid: Enabling Scalable Virtual Organizations, International J. Supercomputer Applications, 15(3), 2001.
5. K. Hosanagar, Krishnan, R., Chuang, J., "Pricing and Service Adoption of Content Delivery Networks (CDNs)", Proceedings of the Hawaii International Conference on Systems and Sciences (HICSS), Hawaii, January 2004.
6. K. Hosanagar, J. Chuang, R. Krishnan, V. Choudhary, "Pricing and Resource Allocation in Caching Services with Multiple Levels of QoS", Management Science, Vol. 51, No. 12, December 2005.
7. Kevin Lai, Bernardo A. Huberman and Leslie Fine, "Tycoon: A Distributed Market-based Resource Allocation Systems", Technical Report arXiv:cs.DC/0404013, April 5, 2004.

8. E. Koutsoupias and C. H. Papadimitriou ``Worst-case equilibria," STACS 1999.
9. A. W. Mu'alem and D. G. Feitelson, "Utilization, predictability, workloads, and user runtime estimates in scheduling the IBM SP2 with backfilling". IEEE Trans. Parallel & Distributed Syst. 12(6), pp. 529–543, Jun 2001.
10. O. Regev and N. Nisan. The Popcorn Market: Online Markets for Computational Resources. In Proceedings of 1st International Conference on Information and Computation Economies, pages 148–157, 1998.
11. C. A. Waldspurger, T. Hogg, B. A. Huberman, J. O. Kephart, and W. S. Stornetta. Spawn: A Distributed Computational Economy. Software Engineering, 18(2):103–117, 1992.
12. M. P. Wellman, W. E. Walsh, P. R. Wurman, and J. K. MacKie-Mason. Auction Protocols for Decentralized Scheduling. Games and Economic Behavior, 35:271–303, 2001.
13. R. Wolski, J.S. Plank, J. Brevik and T.Bryan, Analysing Market-based Resource Allocation Strategies for the Computational Grid International Journal of High-Performance Computing Applications, 15(3), 2001.

A GRID MARKET FRAMEWORK

HING-YAN LEE, THONG-TIONG CHOO, JON LAU KHEE-ERNG & W C WONG
National Grid Office
21 Heng Mui Keng Terrace
Singapore 119613

We outline a proposed framework for a grid market where grid resources can be supplied and acquired in Singapore. While several types of participants already exist, these and other roles that have been identified will evolve over time. The underlying building blocks are being developed to realize the Grid Exchange, which forms the heart of the grid market. We discuss the current version of the framework using the digital media industry as an example and prior work leading to its realization.

1. Introduction

1.1. *National Grid Phase 2*

In the second phase of the National Grid initiative, the focus is on raising awareness and promoting adoption of Grid Computing by business and industry users. The approach taken is sector-based, starting with the digital media vertical.

1.2. *Digital Industry in Singapore*

The Media 21 blueprint envisions Singapore as a Global Media City where media services and projects are created, developed, traded and distributed to the world. The vision also envisages Singapore as Asia's leading media marketplace and financing hub, producing high quality content and digital media. Five strategic thrusts have been articulated towards the realization of the Media 21 vision. They are: establish Singapore as a media exchange; export made-by-Singapore content; deploy digital media; internationalize Singapore media enterprises; and augment media talent. Media 21 expects the industry to grow to US$33 billion by 2008 [1].

While the Media Development Authority (MDA) champions Media 21, the Infocomm and Media (ICM) services cluster promoted by the Economic Development Board (EDB) comprises three sub-clusters: IT, computing and ebusiness; communications; and media and digital entertainment. 2004 saw broad-based growth across all ICM sectors, particularly in games, digital animation and mobile communications. The cluster's projects are the second largest contributor to total business spending under EDB-promoted services clusters. And in digital animation, Singapore secured a landmark project with Lucasfilm's announcement to set up Lucasfilm Animation Singapore, the company's first studio outside of its native California and Singapore's first digital animation studio by an Oscar-winning company. The studio is expected to hire up to 300 animators and will produce digital content for films, television and games for the global audience. Lucasfilm's presence is not only a great boost to the local digital animation sector but has helped to raise Singapore's profile in this industry in the global arena. Singapore aims to increase the GDP contribution of the media cluster from 1.56 per cent to 3 per cent in 10 years, while creating over 10,000 new jobs for Singaporeans.

Under Infocomm Development Authority (IDA)'s Digital Exchange initiative, computer animation has been identified as a key ICT enabler for Digital Media.

1.3 *Grid Computing in Digital Media*

The digital media community has been identified as an industry sector that will reap the low hanging fruits of provisioning computational resources and application software on a pay-per-use or utility basis.

Several efforts to promote a utility-based approach for animation rendering to benefit the digital media industry were initiated in the last year. While these projects take separate paths (clusters vs. Grid Computing), they address common issues crucial to the eventual implementation and successful deployment of the utility-base approach.

Such projects seek to assess the readiness of small and medium sized enterprises (or SMEs) to tap on compute resources from third parties. Their details can be found in the sections on Current Status and Related Work. The positive feedback received has encouraged us to plan for a more ambitious roll-out of provisioning the compute and software resources under the proposed Grid Market Framework (to be described below).

Concurrent with the framework are two new initiatives. The first initiative focuses on the provisioning of commercial animation rendering licenses for Grid Service Providers (GSPs) for use by the digital media industry, while the second initiative helps local digital media companies to build their own enterprise animation rendering grids. Building enterprise grids will enable local digital media companies to better harness their existing computational resources for animation rendering, before they tap on those made available by GSPs. These two initiatives are complementary as the latter may be necessary in some SMEs before they tap on the former. The expected benefits for the digital media community including the following:

- Removes need for hefty upfront investment for hardware and software;
- Reduces need to hire systems staff to administer and operate IT resources;
- Provides benefits of using latest versions of hardware and software, as and when upgrades are available;
- Provides access to a large pool of compute resources on a usage-basis;
- Enables a shorter-time-to-market for products & services; and
- Reduces the Total Cost of Ownership of compute resources.

These benefits are particularly pertinent to the SMEs in Singapore, than to the larger companies and MNCs.

2. Grid Market Framework

The diagram depicts a general framework for a Grid Exchange where compute resource trading takes place and the various players involved. It uses the example of the Grid Exchange serving Users from the Digital Media industry sector.

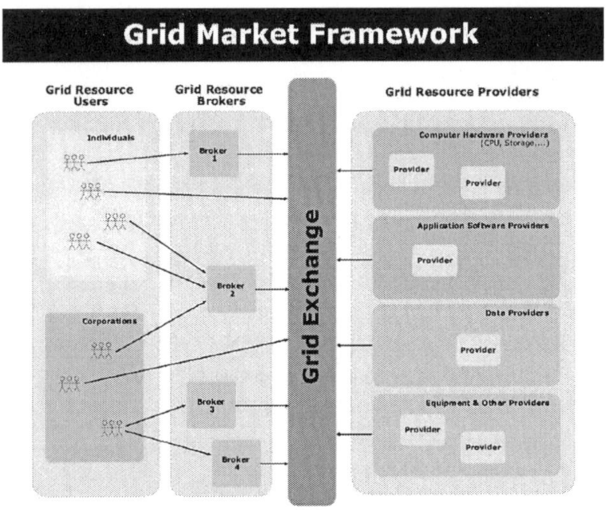

Figure 1: Grid Market Framework

2.1 *Grid Exchange*

A regulatory agency will mediate, engender trust in system, handle crises, etc. It will also be a trusted intermediary that may handle payments & accounts. It manifests itself as a well-known location where buyers and sellers converge as well as provides information and market directories. In the nascent stage, the National Grid will have to take on the role of Grid Exchange until a dedicated entity has been established or identified for this purpose.

While we are unaware of any existing architecture for such a Grid Exchange, there are some foundational building blocks that must be provided to support the activities of compute resource trading.

2.2 *Resource Owners*

These are organizations that own compute resources and who are prepared to make excess, idle or unused capacity available to other users for an agreed price. Some organizations may explicitly provide the resources as their primary business. They could be private corporations, business continuity providers, data centers and ICT vendors.

2.2.1 Compute Resources

In general, such resources include CPUs, storage space, databases, datasets, instruments and sensors made available by Resource Owners.

2.2.2 Applications & Software

Projects and efforts are in progress to jell with the provisioning of applications and software resources. Open source software such as BLAST and POV-Ray [2] are presently available on the National Grid Pilot Platform (NGPP). While in-house developed software also do not pose any problem other than the need to grid-enable them, licensing issues of commercial software and applications are potential show-stoppers.

2.3 *Grid Resource Brokers (GRBs)*

These entities interface with Users and help them fulfil their need for both computational and software resources by mediating with Resource Owners. They can take the form of real companies that have established themselves to play such a role. Or as envisaged in the computing literature, they manifest themselves as software agents that seek to fulfil a user's requirement through online negotiation with agents from Resource Owners, subject to technical requirements, specified budget and/or deadline constraints.

2.4 *Users*

Users are consumers of compute resources. In the digital media industry, there are currently some 50 or so animation and gaming SMEs in Singapore which are potential beneficiaries, the majority of these are small. They often do not have ready access to large compute resources and high quality animation software to tap on. This shortcoming, in turn, hampers their desire to take on large and/or high value jobs.

2.5 *Grid Service Providers (GSPs)*

Such entities take on roles of Resource Owners and/or GRBs. They may own some resources and where needed, broker with other Resource Owners to help users fulfill their computational needs.

3. Current Status of Deployment

3.1 The Current Players

Compute Resources

To kick off the initiative, the computational resources from the present NGPP have been made available to provide a heterogeneous setting. Specifically, these are a 72-CPU Xeon cluster and a 78-CPU Itanium-2 cluster.

Grid Service Providers

The ideal situation is one where "a thousand flowers blossom" because there is indeed a market for Grid services to sustain their business. In reality, the business case has to be made and internalized by the digital media SMEs. To this end, we have been nurturing and promoting two such GSPs.

Applications & Software

The availability of software licenses is a critical success factor. The NGPP has been installed with POV-Ray [2] and Cel-Animation [3] to form a digital media grid that is open to interested parties to experience running animation rendering jobs. More importantly to digital media SMEs is the access to high-quality third party proprietary animation rendering software. The extent of success that we can achieve will depend on how willing software vendors are prepared to evolve their licensing schemes to make them viable for Grid Computing. Hitherto, some successes have been achieved.

Together with the IDA and MDA, we completed a proof-of-concept where a common pool of 150 mental ray [4] licenses software was made available to several local digital media SMEs over a period of three months. During this trial, the companies participated by testing the readiness and robustness of the interface between the front-end modeling tools (like Maya and 3DStudioMax) and the rendering back-end, the need for file format conversions, and performance issues. Since then, we have provision the mental ray commercial licenses for the SMEs in Singapore. We expect to close similar arrangements for the animation rendering software with other software vendors.

Enterprise Grids

In addition, we have also embarked upon a scheme to help the local digital media SMEs to build enterprise grids as a stepping stone to tap on compute resources on the NGPP.

One of the very first digital media companies that we worked with is digital media hub (dmh). dmh is a centre for the development and advancement of digital media, which provides facilities encapsulating the entire value chain of film making - from pre-production, production, post-production to distribution. A joint effort was undertaken to network existing PCs in dmh into a rendering grid in late 2005. dmh has since successfully put their rendering grid to good use, including using them for training by the digital media academy (dma), which is housed in dmh.

dmh then faces a situation that many digital media companies are familiar with – their internal compute resources are insufficient for the many rendering jobs piling up with extremely tight deadlines. Some of the software owned by dma are only for training purpose and cannot be used for commercial projects. To resolve this, huge investments would need to be made. Efficient utilization of the acquired hardware and software is a challenge in between projects.

dmh decided to tap onto compute resources on the NGPP to help them address their rendering needs in the most effective manner. Other digital companies that are exploring include VHQ and Omen Studios.

Users have different preferences on how to use the software licenses and the resources on NGPP. Some prefer to use a front-end modeling software such as Maya or 3D Studio Max, which have a more friendly user-interface, to execute the rendering process for their images. Some of the more technically inclined users prefer to export the images into the rendering software's file format, or a standard file format such as the RIB format, and use scripts for rendering. If animator has sufficient compute resources of his own, he can check out the licenses and run them using his compute resources. If additional compute resources are required, he can tap onto resources on NGPP or other sources.

3.2 Realizing the GMH

The development of the GMH is a huge undertaking and will require the participation and contributions of many in the Grid community. Towards putting in place the components that are necessary to realize the GMH, we have begun identifying several basic components and deploying them.

Some of the components that are already in place on the NGPP include Multi-organization Grid Accounting System, Netrust Certificate Authority (CA), and Load Sharing Facility (LSF) Meta Scheduler.

3.2.1 Multi-organization Grid Accounting System (MOGAS)

MOGAS [13] aims to address the need to log and account for the resource usage across a grid of heterogeneous compute resources made available by their owners for access by users from within and without their organization. In such a setting, the resource owners want to log and review the sharing of resources among the different organizations.

MOGAS currently supports N1GE, LSF and PBS workload schedulers. Work is in progress to interface MOGAS with the LSF Meta Scheduler. A portal is available to provide access to view the data. Its features include:

- Tabulated display of inter-organization sharing of resources;
- View based on organization, project and individual users; and
- Billing.

Its development commenced in August 2004. The latest version, MOGAS v3.0, has been deployed across the Nanyang Campus Grid, NGPP, and several sites on the PRAGMA test-bed [12].

3.2.2 Netrust Certificate Authority

To ensure that the CA is robust and scalable, we have appointed a commercial entity, Netrust Pte Ltd, to handle the issuing and management of the digital certificates for compute hosts and users on the National Grid in Singapore.

While the creation of digital certificates could be accomplished by using public source certificate generation tool (e.g. simpleCA), the level of security implemented is dependent on the processes for checking the identity of the user or host before issuing the certificate, and also the extent to which the root key is stored. These are processes stated in the Certificate Policies (CP) and the Certification Practice Statement (CPS). It is the CP and CPS that constitute a basis for the accreditation of a CA. This effort entails the migration from free digital certificates to commercial CA digital certificates so as to:

- Increase security robustness, in preparation for industry focus in NGPP

- Understand security procedures & issues pertaining to commercial CA certificate

NGPP sites nominate representatives to receive digital certificates. As of today, all NGPP sites have migrated their host certificates to Netrust certificates.

3.2.3 LSF Meta-Scheduler

The deployment of a meta-scheduler arose from the need for a general scheduler to ease the submission and scheduling of jobs to the NGPP resources. Since each of the NGPP resources has its own local workload schedulers (such as Sun's N1GE and Platform's LSF), the need to find a scheduler that could interface to these local schedulers is important and necessary. The NGPP meta-scheduler, in the form of the LSF Meta-Scheduler from Platform Computing, was deployed by end 2005.

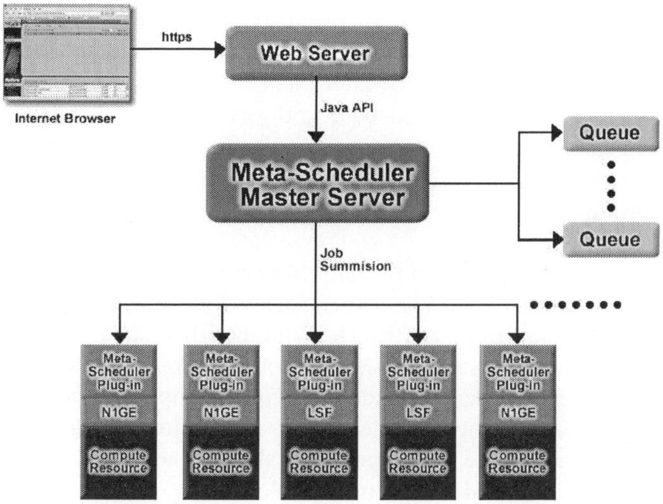

Figure 2: NGPP Meta-Scheduler Architecture

The meta-scheduler has a web interface that allows users to submit and monitor jobs sent to the NGPP resources. This provides users an easier and more intuitive interface as compared to the command-line interface which the meta-scheduler also provides.

Other components that make up the GMH would include systems similar to those such as GridASP [9], Sun Grid [10], and Tycoon [11].

4. Related Work

Under the Adaptive Enterprise @ Singapore (AE@SG) collaboration initiative between IDA and HP, the Nanyang Technological University (NTU), Singapore Management University (SMU), Institute of High Performance Computing (IHPC) and HP Labs are co-developing a suite of solutions that would ease the use of Grid Computing by animators. A user council comprising representatives from digital media SMEs and ICT companies has been established to provide requirements and ensure that solutions will be usable.

Concurrent with the AE@SG effort, the IDA, Managed Computing Competency Centre, the Digital Media Chapter of the Singapore ICT Federation, as well as local and international companies completed a concept prototype for a virtual remote rendering facility. As a next step, the facility will be linked up with NGPP to extend collective resources for an animation rendering environment.

Buyya et al [5] presented a computational economy as a model for addressing the challenges of resource management in large-scale grids based on commodity market based resource allocation. The model, *inter alia*, includes scheduling in computational and data grid environments as well as auction models applied to resource trading.

5. Conclusions

In this paper, we have presented the Grid Market Hub (GMH) framework that is being deployed in phases. We plan to apply the same framework in other verticals like manufacturing, and R&D. With the IHPC and i-Math Pte Ltd, we have conducted a trial using the FEMLAB software, for multi-physics modeling and analyses in diverse science and engineering disciplines, such as structural mechanics, chemical engineering, electronics, and electromagnetic, on a pay-per-use model using the above framework. We also plan to conduct trials software from MSC.Software and Matlab from MathWorks.

Acknowledgments

This paper has benefited from discussions with Jason Tan (Hewlett-Packard Singapore), Simon See (Asia Pacific Science & Technology Centre, Sun Microsystems), Francis Lee, (NTU), Steve Miller (SMU), Ronnie Lee and Ng Wan Sin (IDA), and Yeo Chun Cheng (MDA).

References

1. The Roncarelli Report on Computer Animation Industry, 2003.
2. POV-Ray. http://www.povray.org/
3. Hock-Soon Seah and Tian Feng. Computer-Assisted Coloring by Matching Line Drawings, The Visual Computer, Vol. 16, 2000, pp. 289-304.
4. Mental Ray from mental images GmbH.
5. Rajkumar Buyya, David Abramson, and Srikumar Venugopal. The Grid Economy, Proc. IEEE, Vol. 93, No. 3, March 2005.
6. FEMLAB. www.comsol.com.
7. MSC.Software. http://www.mscsoftware.com/.
8. Matlab. http://www.mathworks.com/.
9. Satoshi Itoh, Hirotaka Ogawa, Tetsuya Sonoda and Satoshi Sekiguchi. GridASP – A Framework for a New Utility Business, Proc. 2nd International Workshop on Grid Economics & Business Models, Seoul, South Korea, 13 March 2005.
10. Sun Grid. http://www.sun.com/service/sungrid/overview.jsp.
11. Kevin Lai, L. Rasmusson, S. Sorkin, L. Zhang, and Bernardo A. Huberman. Tycoon: An Implementation of a Distributed Market-Based Resource Allocation System, HP Labs Palo Alto, Technical Report, 4 December 2004.
12. PRAGMA. http://www.pragma-grid.net/.
13. Hee-Khiang Ng, Quoc-Thuan Ho, B-Sung Lee, Dudy Lim, Yew-Soon Ong and Wentong Cai. Nanyang Campus Inter-Organization Grid Monitoring System, Proc. GridAsia Workshop on Grid Computing & Applications, Singapore, May 2005.

A MARKET-BASED FRAMEWORK FOR TRADING GRID RESOURCES

MELVIN KOH, JIE SONG, LIANG PENG AND SIMON SEE

Asia Pacific Science and Technology Center,
Sun Microsystems Inc.
Advance Design and Modelling Laboratory,
Nanyang Technological University,
50 Nanyang Avenue, Singapore 639798

Grid computing is recognized as a potential major platform for scientific computing as well as commercial computation in the future. However, despite the existing technical advances and commercial needs, up till now, almost all research efforts are focused on using Grids within academic community. The adoption of Grid technology by commercial companies has been slow. This is mainly because there is no existing support for chargeable Grid services and commercial transactions on them. To support this, a complete set of mechanisms that enable Grid services to be registered, discovered, negotiated, and paid for the usage are required. In this paper, we propose a framework based on a market-economy approach that will provide the necessary building blocks for commercial implementation of Grid computing business models. We also present a prototype that allow publishing and searching of registered Grid resources and show how it can be use to support the trading of resources in a virtual market.

1. Introduction

Along with the fast increasing demands on computing power by researchers in various areas, the concept of Grid was envisaged in 1990s for virtualizing heterogeneous computing resources to share across different organizations. For enterprises, we expect that Grids will first start to form inside corporate firewalls. After these grids are established, companies will start looking at buying extra capacity on other people's grids or renting out their own surplus computing power. When this happens, there will be a need to have a common place for the companies to trade their resources. This common place function as a virtual marketplace that provides mechanism for advertising resource offerings, searching for suitable resources and negotiating prices. Since, like in real world, each market differs from another, a framework is necessary to allow easy customization and extension.

There could be a number of scenarios of how the Grid market is used. Here we give two typical scenarios.

- Scenario 1: Service Consumer. A manufacturing company has been using traditional applications on their own resources to do stress analysis on the design of new machine parts. In order to minimize the product time-to-market, they need to perform the analysis as fast as possible for this new product and so decide to "buy" services from the Grid Service Market. The company searches for suitable services and with the service requirements as parameters, e.g. expected budget and duration of usage, the Market presents the user with a list of acceptable (or near-acceptable) choices, and iterates with the user on refining the set of parameters. Eventually, after the company is satisfied, it will confirm their choice(s) with the Market and a contract will be sent to both parties for verification and to sign electronically. Once the contract is finalized, the company is allowed to use the services for the duration of the contract.

- Scenario 2: Service Provider. An electronic design automation software vendor has developed Grid service interfaces for their applications and wants to offer them in the Grid Service Market. The company's administrator deploys the charging service together with their application services, and sets up the configuration including the charging prices and schemes. Then, the administrator publishes the services to the Grid Service Market registry so that other users can find them. At every pre-defined period, for example the end of every quarter, the company will retrieve the services usage information from the Market accounting service, and bill their customers accordingly.

The remainder of this paper is organized as follows: In Section 2 we describe some of the research issues that we face in our proposed Grid Market Framework and its architecture. Section 3 presents the design and implementation details of a prototype that will be abstracted to form part of the framework. Related works are discussed in Section 4 and we conclude in the last Section with some future work.

2. Research Issues and Framework Architecture

In order for our framework to be a viable solution, there are several research issues that need to be addressed. First and foremost, there is no known business model that has been applied to the Grid. It is also not known if existing models, like those used for Internet services or power grid, are suitable. Moreover, it may not be sufficient to just have a single model, or restricted charging schemes, that could be employed in the market since different virtual organizations may operate in different ways. It is therefore necessary to investigate and develop mechanisms whereby different models can be realized. In addition, to be able to support a Grid Market infrastructure, other components in the framework, such as service registry and broker, need to be made economic-aware. This means that most of the existing tools cannot be apply directly - they need to be extended or adapted.

Another important issue is the automated negotiation, as the users of a grid service market may not want to handle every detail in service negotiation. Thus, there is a need for using autonomous agents to negotiate on behalf of the users. Currently, the only known effort to standardize the negotiation protocol that serves this purpose is the WS-Agreement initiative [1]. However, it is an on-going effort and the protocol is still in draft stage.

Here we define the basic mechanisms that the Grid Market Framework needs to provide:

- Mechanism for a service consumer to retrieve pricing and service information from a chargeable Grid service.
- Mechanism for service providers to register their services and advertise their capabilities and charging policies.
- Brokering mechanism that performs service discovery and optimize selection according to requirements, incorporating both performance and cost information.
- Mechanism for negotiation between consumers and providers of Grid services. The negotiation should be performed by, for example software agents, using artificial intelligent techniques and game theory to maximize collective utility for both the consumers and providers.

Figure 1 gives the layered overview of the functional components what a complete Grid market framework should have. We are working towards building the components showed in the Grid market layer.

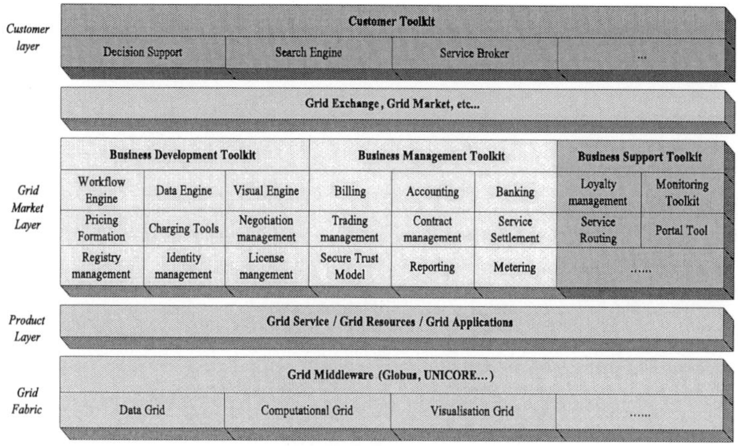

Figure 1. Layered Overview of the Grid Market Framework

3. Prototype Design and Implementation

Our Grid Market Framework project is still in the infancy stage, but as part of our effort in developing the framework, we have implemented a prototype which consists of several components from the layered overview (figure 1).

3.1. *Portal Components*

Figure 2 shows the components of the portal and the backend agents. The agents provide most of the functionality of the portal and are also responsible for interacting with external entities like the Provider and GridBank service. They are implemented using the Jade Agent Toolkit [11].

Currently, the portal provides function for searching, publishing and purchasing of resources. On top of these, it also has the contract management component that allows users to manage their contacts from the web interface. Figure 3 shows a sample screenshot a user sees when searching for a resource providers on the web portal interface.

The portal utilizes a centralized database for storing the information of the providers and the resources they offer. The trading agent searches and filters these information according to the requirements provided by the user. In other words, the trading agent is responsible for getting the list of available resources that the user need. The trading agent also fulfill the roles of the negotiation and trading components in the framework - after obtaining the list of providers that has the required resources, the agent

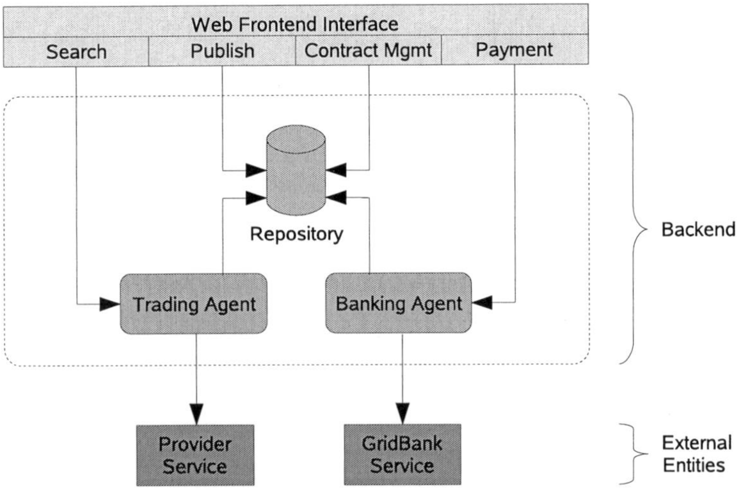

Figure 2. Components of the Portal

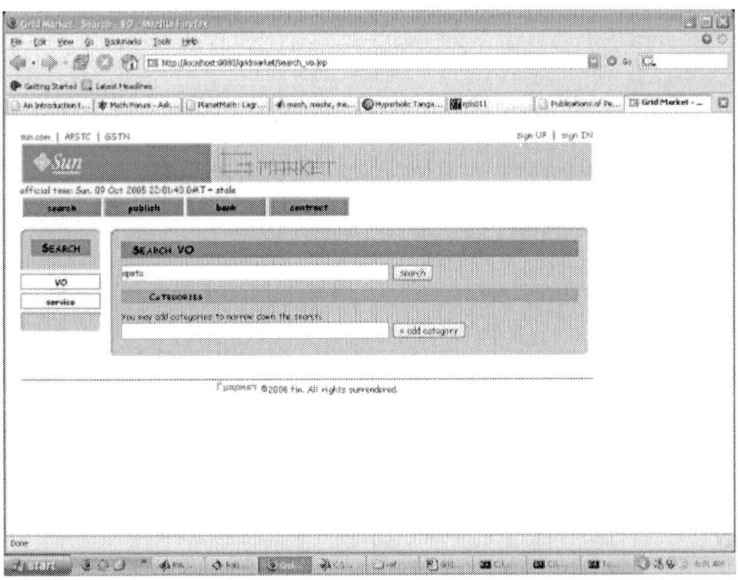

Figure 3. Searching for a Provider

will perform negotiation with the providers on the price.

The billing components of our framework is implemented as a banking agent that facilitates inter-bank communication, which consists of exchanging cheques and drafts as the means of transfer payments. As part of the testbed, we implemented a GridBank service that provides account management and credit transfer mechanisms.

3.2. *GridBank Service*

The GridBank service is implemented as a OGSI Grid service using Globus Toolkit 3, which fulfills on the role of the banking component in our framework. Here we list the requirements that our GridBank service needs to satisfy:

- Must provide account management, such as opening, checking, and closing the account.
- Must facilitate money transfer between Grid Banks.
- Must facilitate the query of a transactions history.
- Must enable currency exchange.
- Must allow the creation of account hold.

The last point is enforced to assure the provider of getting paid after the service duration is over. By holding to the buyer's account, GridBank will automatically refuse any withdrawal that could reduce the balance below the amount hold. The account hold itself is not persistent and has an expiry time. Figure 4 depicts the GridBank class diagram.

The GridBankingService is a persistent Grid service that satisfies all of our requirements. Furthermore, when createHold() is invoked, it will create an instance of GridBankingHoldService, which is defined as a transient Grid service. It has a well-defined termination time which can be prolonged or shortened when the need arises.

4. Related Work

There are some increasing interests in applying economic approaches to Grid computing technology, but the efforts are mainly on developing economy based application schedulers [2,3] and very few of them focus on providing necessary building blocks for commercialization of Grids. Computational economy enables the regulation of supply and demand of resources, offers incentive for resource owners for leasing, and promotes QoS based resource management [4]. The most notable effort of applying computational economy in Grid computing is the Gridbus project lead by Dr Rajkumar Buyya [5]. The GridBus aims at applying some economic rules for better

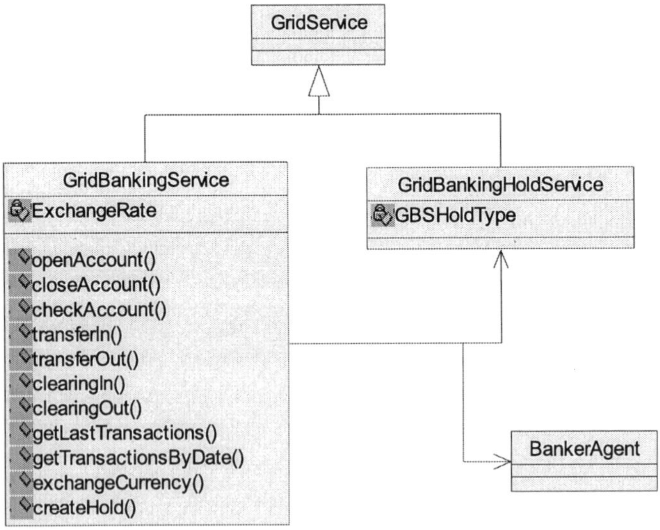

Figure 4. GridBank Services and Operations

Grid resource management. Another is a project under the UK e- Science Programme, which tries to build a Grid Market Architecture for the UK e-Science Grid [6]. There is also a Grid Economics Service Architecture Working Group (GESA-WG) under the Global Grid Forum (GGF) [7]. Business Grid [8] is a project supported by Japan's Ministry of Economy, Trade and Industry (METI), which involves Fujitsu, NEC and AIST. Their work collaborates with independent software vendors (ISVs) and resource providers in order to drive utility computing in Japan. There are also several other new projects, for instance, the ChinaGrid [9], which are also working on applying economics for resource management. In Shanghai Grid project, a Grid accounting system has been developed, which consists three functionality parts: the usage information collecting system, the records processing system, and the charging system [10]. However, in spite of these efforts, an experimental Grid market platform is still not yet available.

5. Conclusion and Future Work

In this paper, we highlight that the adoption of Grid techonology in the industry is still very slow compared to the academic and research community. We also note that if there is a means for commercial companies to sell or buy extra resources using Grid technology, it will definitely speed up the process. Thus a framework will be needed to support the commercialization of Grid resources, and we present the functional components that are required to build such a complete Grid market environment. As part of our preliminary work, we introduced our prototype implementation that currently consists of an agent-based system with a portal frontend and a Grid banking service.

We want to emphasize that there is a lot of work still to be done. For example, the negotiation portion is still missing. For this, we will be implementing an agent to be deployed by the provider which negotiates with the trading agent on a suitable price. Another future work is that we also want to try out different charging models. The most common way to charge is using a utility model, which charge customers only by the amount used. However, this may be inflexible and difficult to predict how much resources will be used. Other models like leasing or subscription-based may be more appropriate, or perhaps a simple fixed price will suffice.

Acknowledgements

The Grid Market prototype is implemented by Endang Purwanto Sulaiman during his industrial attachment with APSTC. The authors thank him and his supervisor, Dr Ong Yew Soon, for their contributions.

References

1. A. Andrieux, C. Czajkowski, A. Dan, K. Keahey, H. Ludwig, J. Pruyne, J. Rofrano, S. Tuecke, M. Xu. Web Services Agreement Specification (WS-Agreement). Version 1.1, Draft 20, June 6th 2004.
2. User-centric Performance Analysis of Market-based Cluster Batch Schedulers, by Brent N. Chun and David E. Culler, in Procs. of the 2nd IEEE/ACM International Symposium on Cluster Computing and Grid (CCGrid), 2002.
3. g-Commerce: Market Formulations Controlling Resource Allocation on the Computational Grid, by R. Wolski, J. S. Plank and J. Brevik, in Procs. of International Parallel and Distributed Processing Symposium, San Francisco, CA, USA, April 2001.
4. Spawn: A Distributed Computational Economy, by C. Waldspurger, T. Hogg, B. Huberman, J. Kephard and W. Stornetta, in IEEE Transactions on Software Engineering, 8(2):103-117, Feb 1992.
5. Economic Models for Resource Management and Scheduling in Grid Computing, by Rajkumar Buyya, David Abramson, Jonathan Giddy, and Heinz Stockinger, Special Issue on Grid Computing Environments, in The Journal of Concurrency and Computation: Practice and Experience, 14(13-15): 1507-1542, Wiley Press, USA, November - December 2002.

6. Trading Grid Services Within The UK E-Science Grid, Steven Newhouse, Jon MacLaren, and Katarzyna Keahey, Book Chapter, Grid Resource Management C State of the Art and Future Trends(page 479-490), edited by Jarek Nabrzyski, Jennifer M. Schopf, and Jan Weglarz, Kluwer Academic Publishers, 2004.
7. Grid Economic Services Architecture Working Group, Global Grid Forum, http://www.doc.ic.ac.uk/ sjn5/GGF/GESA-WG3.htm
8. Business Grid Middleware, Hiro Kishimoto, Fujitsu, Japan, http://www.globusworld.org/program/slides/3c_1.pdf
9. The Overview of ChinaGrid, Hai Jin, HUST, China. http://unpan1.un.org/intradoc/groups/public/documents/APCITY/UNPAN016934.pdf
10. A Service-Oriented Accounting Architecture on the Grid , by Jiadi Yu, Minglu Li, Ying Li, Feng Hong and Yujun Du, in Procs. of 5th International Conference on Parallel and Distributed Computing: Applications and Technologies (PDCAT), Singapore, Dec 2004.
11. JADE: A FIPA-compliant agent framework, F. Bellifemine, A. Poggi, and G. Rimassi, in Proceedings of the Practical Applications of Intelligent Agents and Multi-Agents, April 1999, pp. 97–108.

Pricing, Charging & Accounting Issues of Heterogeneous Resources

TARIFF STRUCTURES FOR PRICING GRID COMPUTING RESOURCES

H. K. BHARGAVA AND A. BAGH
University of California Davis
Davis, CA 95616
email: {hemantb, abagh}@ucdavis.edu

Multi-part tariffs are quite popular in the information, communication, and entertainment industries. These include two-part tariffs (fixed membership fee, plus per-use fee), three-part tariffs (fixed fee, allowance level, per-use fee), flat-rate tariffs (fixed fee, unlimited use), linear tariffs, progressive tariffs (initial rate up to some level, then higher rate), etc. We discuss the role of these structures in a market for grid computing resources under a utility computing model. We also analyze connection between pricing and capacity planning under demand uncertainty and information asymmetry.

1. Introduction

Grid computing technologies [7, 10] provide transparent access to large-scale computing power by bringing together a heterogeneous collection of computational resources (computation, information, database, storage, bandwidth, etc.) through the Internet. A variety of scientific and society-oriented non-commercial applications already exploit such technologies, notable examples are GriPhyN [6], SETI@home, and computation-intensive research such as earthquake simulation and drug discovery [1]. There has been tremendous progress in standardization, virtualization, and other aspects of grid technologies [8, 9, 2, 11]. This technological maturity has fueled investments in an "on-demand" or "utility" computing model for business computing, one where commercial business applications run, in part, on network-based resources dynamically provisioned off a computing grid.

Grid economics is concerned with resource allocation (who gets how much? [4]), scheduling (when? [15]), pricing (who pays, for how much? [3]) and resource planning (how much capacity, when to commit?). This paper primarily examines the last two questions, of price design and capacity planning, which are critical ingredients for large-scale use of grid technologies in business computing. For instance, major IT suppliers are looking for suitable ways to measure and price computational resources (e.g., Sun Microsystems's *power units*, IBM's *service units*, and Hewlett-Packard's *computons*). Our work has two key elements. First, it analyzes and compares *types of pricing structures* for grid computing, rather than merely the optimal pricing policy within one structure. Second, our research explores the connections between the choice of pricing structure and capacity planning, demonstrating that a well-chosen price structure can lead to better decisions on capacity. For simplicity, we adopt the term "computon" as a generic representative of different types of computational resources.

2. Economic Framework

Business applications running on a grid require not just computons, but additional guarantees and safeguards pertaining to their use (rather than, say, "best-effort" service). The computon, therefore, is not a commodity which business customers can procure directly from a grid supplied by small, unknown resource owners. Instead, we envision that customers will trade with computing vendors of repute, probably have brand preferences, and care about quality of service, speed, accuracy, data privacy, security, etc. Thus, computons will not be costless to supply, and competition between computon suppliers will not drive price to zero. In order to supply customer demand that is potentially volatile and unpredictable (see below), computing vendors might deploy grid computing technologies over an internal collection of computons, or perhaps over an external collection involving downstream suppliers. From the customer's perspective, however, there is a single vendor, who must manage pricing with the customer(s), map tasks to resources, and manage the downstream supply chain to procure sufficient computons. Our perspective implies the following specific model features.

Supply The computing vendor will incur non-negligible costs, both fixed and variable, in arranging computon capacity with requisite guarantees. Vendors might pre-commit to some capacity level at a unit variable cost c_1, and arrange additional on-demand capacity at a higher unit cost c_2.

Demand The customer faces a computational task which requires an uncertain quantity of computons to complete, this quantity $\tilde{q}$ is a draw from a known distribution. The customer's willingness-to-pay is

$V(q)$ for q computons, and may be interpreted as the cost of the outside alternative adjusted for the vendor's brand premium. In general, the marginal WTP $V_q(q)$ will vary with q, most likely with diminishing marginal gains. Demand uncertainty is a crucial aspect of a grid computing market. As noted in *The Economist* (March 12, 2005), businesses "do not think of their computing needs in terms of, say, 50 processor-hours; instead, they ... want to get those tasks done economically, using whatever resources are available."

2.1. *Demand Uncertainty and Information Asymmetry*

Our framework involves both *demand uncertainty*—neither vendor nor customer know the exact number of computons required to finish a task—and *information asymmetry*—the buyer knows the task, but the seller knows only the overall distribution of tasks and not the task faced by each buyer. This one-buyer framework is identical to a multi-buyer framework in which each buyer has a certain type of task (which determines the distribution for resource requirement), each buyer knows her own type, but the seller knows only the overall distribution of buyers and not the type of each buyer.

The combination of demand uncertainty and information asymmetry poses a particular challenge in designing pricing models for computing resources. The vendor has a lower cost for planned capacity than for on-demand capacity (so, $c_1 \leq c_2$), faces pressure to supply an uncertain quantity of resources, but must plan its supply without less information than the buyer has about the distribution of the uncertain demand quantity. Simply asking the buyer doesn't work, because the buyer has an incentive to exaggerate her needs. This implies a pricing mechanism which provides buyers an incentive to reveal their private information. Thus, our framework allows vendors to set a non-refundable fee for advance reservation, and customers to choose an advance reservation capacity. Advance reservation is recognized as a technological necessity and is present in several grid designs [14], we find that it (i.e., a fee for reservation) is also economically desirable.

2.2. *Tariff Structures*

Following the above discussion, we analyze two general contractual schemes.

2.2.1. *Three-Part Tariff*

The seller announces (F, Q, p). A customer who accepts this tariff commits a fixed fee F for utilization level (or allowance) Q, and has an option to use additional units at a unit price p. The seller announces (F, Q, p), and the customer's choice is to accept or reject the contract. Well-known special cases of three-part tariffs include (a) linear "pay as you go" tariffs ($Q = 0, F = 0$), (b) flat-rate "all you can eat" tariffs ($Q = \infty$ or $p = 0$), and (c) two-part tariffs (with $Q = 0, F = V$), pay-as-you-go after an access fee. Pay as you go tariffs have been a critical ingredient in the marketing of utility computing and related models for business computing (e.g., application hosting, data center outsourcing, web hosting), and flat-rate tariffs are popular in computing and communications, in part due to a "flat-rate bias" exhibited by consumers and business customers [12, 13].

When customers know their demand level, the three-part tariff is a special case of nonlinear pricing (a menu of quantity-price pairs), nevertheless it is a strong alternative to nonlinear pricing due to simplicity. As noted by a potential customer of utility-computing (ComputerWorld, May 26, 2005), "The last thing that we need is another complicated licensing scheme ... What we need is a quick and easy way to buy more computing power, and I need to be able to buy it in very small, inexpensive increments." As the second part of the quote demonstrates, the other attractive feature of a three-part (or of a two-part) tariff structure is flexibility regarding total consumption level. In contrast, a nonlinear price menu requires the customer to commit consumption level in advance, therefore the customer would be unable to select the best pair from the menu (because she does not know her exact resource requirement), and the seller lacks information for designing the optimal menu.

2.2.2. *Progressive Co-designed Tariff*

The second scheme is a progressive tariff in which the seller announces a price pair (p_1, p_2) and the buyer commits a consumption level Q in response. The contract commits the buyer to a fixed fee $p_1 Q$ (representing a unit price p_1 up to consumption level Q) and allows the buyer to consume additional units at a per-unit price p_2. The buyer chooses Q to maximize her surplus, given prices p_1 and p_2. This tariff may be written as a three-part tariff $(p_1 Q, Q, p_2)$, subject to the buyer's choice of Q and $p_1 < p_2$. However, it is a "co-designed" tariff—it explicitly involves the buyer in tariff design—a mechanism that is capable of providing incentives to the more informed party to reveal useful information in exchange for a fee. the seller under information asymmetry. Related price structures include block-declining or tapered tariffs in which $p_2 < p_1$ [5], but these do not involve the customer in price design.

3. Model

We formalize our model below and present an analysis of results, following which we elaborate on its implications for the suitability of different price structures.

3.1. *The Buyers*

The market has a heterogeneous collection of buyers. Each buyer's type, denoted by $\theta \in \Theta$, is private information to the buyer, and the seller knows only the distribution of θ. Alternately, we can view the market as consisting of one buyer with type θ, where the seller only knows the distribution of θ. A type θ buyer expects to have a computational task τ_θ for which she has a maximum willingness-to-pay $V(\theta)$ but is uncertain about the task or its resource requirement. Thus, type θ buyer requires q computons where q is a random variable over $[0, b(\theta)]$ with a pdf $\phi_\theta(q)$ and a cdf $\Phi_\theta(q)$. Table 1 describes some scenarios representing task uncertainty and corresponding buyer valuation. For the first two cases in the table, the buyer would accept a contract which accomplishes the task with an expected payment $R(\theta)$ less than $V(\theta)$. The current paper focuses on this case. For case 3, the customer would accept a contract in the same way, but would also make a second decision to terminate the computation if resource utilization exceeds some maximum threshold level $\hat{Q}$. The function V satisfies the usual property of diminishing marginal returns, so $V_\theta(\theta) > 0$ while $V_{\theta\theta}(\theta) \leq 0$.

Evaluation of Three-Part Tariff If the seller offers a three-part tariff (F, Q, p), the buyer signs the following contract *before* the realization of the random variable q: Pay a fixed fee F and receive Q computons; Pay p per unit for any consumption over Q. For the initial exposition of this problem, we assume that for agent θ, q is uniformly distributed over $[0, b(\theta)]$ so that $\phi(q) = \frac{1}{b(\theta)}$. A type θ buyer gets utility $V(\theta)$ from the service, and faces a total tariff

$$T(\theta) = F + \frac{p}{b(\theta)} \int_Q^{b(\theta)} (q - Q)dq$$

1. Uncertainty in scale of task. Firm X wants to use computing resources for an accounting task. It will transfer vendor a series of accounting database transactions for the quarter. These transactions need to be processed and turned into the firm's quarterly profit and loss statement. The task's resource requirements will depend on the number of transactions n, about which the firm is uncertain, for example it may have 10 million transactions or 5 million. The firm's WTP for this task is an expected value derived as

$$V = \int_a^b V(n)dF(n)$$

where $F(n)$ is the cdf of the number of transactions (over an interval $[a, b]$), and $V(n)$ is the firm's WTP conditional on the task containing n transactions.

2. Uncertainty in task complexity with "All or no" valuation of effort. Firm Y has a complex computational problem requiring the execution of an advanced heuristic to determine a feasible schedule for N jobs with M constraints. The heuristic may find such a schedule within 1 minute or, perhaps, it might run for an hour. Y's valuation for this task, however, is independent of how long it might take to solve the problem.

3. Uncertainty in task complexity with partial valuation of effort. Firm Z wants to run data mining algorithms to find interesting patterns on a massive terrabyte data set, with patterns scored according to a specified fitness measure. It expects the algorithms to run for several hours, and produce a trend of increasingly interesting patterns. The algorithms are to be run until the fitness scores reach a pre-specified convergence pattern. Z's willingness-to-pay is V if the algorithm converges or consumes resources $\hat{Q}$. For resources $q < \hat{Q}$. Z's valuation is a monotonically increasing function $V(q)$, where q represents quantity of computation on the task, with $V_q > 0$ and $V_{qq} < 0$.

Figure 1. Some scenarios representing uncertainty in computational task and resource requirements for the task.

The buyer accepts the contract if and only if

$$V(\theta) - T(\theta) \geq 0 \tag{1}$$

The set of buyers follows the usual properties (that higher types get higher allocations) if $T(\theta) - V(\theta)$ is increasing in θ. Computing the derivative of this term yields a sufficient condition:

$$\frac{V_\theta(\theta)}{b_\theta(\theta)} - \frac{p}{2} + \frac{pQ^2}{b(\theta)^2} \geq 0 \quad \forall\theta \tag{2}$$

This yields the intuitive property that higher types get higher surplus as long as the variable rate p is low, Q is high, or $V(\theta)$ increases faster than $b(\theta)$. When this regularity condition holds there is an indifferent type $\hat{\theta}$ such that types in $[\hat{\theta}, 1]$ purchase the service while those in $[0, \hat{\theta}]$ do not. Specifically,

$$\hat{\theta} \text{ is the solution to } V(\theta) = \left(F + \frac{p}{b(\theta)} \int_Q^{b(\theta)} (q - Q)dq\right).$$

Evaluation of Co-Designed Tariff If the seller offers a progressive tariff (p_1, p_2), and the buyer chooses a commitment quantity Q (hence a price commitment $p_1 Q$, yielding the following expected tariff:

$$T(\theta) = p_1 Q + \frac{p_2}{b(\theta)} \int_Q^{b(\theta)} (q - Q)dq$$

A type θ buyer chooses an optimal commitment level Q^* by solving the following optimization problem.

$$\max_{Q \in [0, b(\theta)]} V(\theta) - \left(p_1 Q + \frac{p_2}{b(\theta)} \int_Q^{b(\theta)} (q - Q)dq\right) \tag{3}$$

which yields

$$Q^*(\theta) = \alpha_1 b(\theta) \tag{4}$$

where

$$\alpha_1 = \frac{p_2 - p_1}{p_2} \tag{5}$$

Substituting into $T(\theta)$ we get the expected tariff payment as

$$T(\theta) = \frac{p_1(p_2 - 0.5p_1)}{p_2} b(\theta) = \alpha_2 b(\theta)$$

where

$$\alpha_2 = \frac{p_1(p_2 - 0.5p_1)}{p_2} \tag{6}$$

Type θ gets a positive surplus so long as

$$\frac{V(\theta)}{b(\theta)} > \alpha_2$$

which is type θ's participation constraint. Moreover, If (p_1, p_2) are chosen such that $\frac{V_\theta(\theta)}{b_\theta(\theta)} > \alpha_2$, then we can get the needed regularity condition that higher types get greater surplus. A simple sufficiency condition for this is that $\frac{V(\theta)}{b(\theta)}$ is weakly increasing in θ (that is, $\frac{V_\theta}{V(\theta)} \geq \frac{b_\theta}{b(\theta)}$). Under this condition, there is an indifferent type $\hat{\theta}$ such that types in $[\hat{\theta}, 1]$ purchase the service while those in $[0, \hat{\theta}]$ do not. Specifically,

$$\hat{\theta} \text{ is the solution to } \frac{V(\theta)}{b(\theta)} = \frac{p_1(p_2 - 0.5p_1)}{p_2}.$$

Last, note that this co-designed contract is equivalent to the three-part tariff $(p_1\alpha_1 b(\theta), \alpha_1 b(\theta), p_2)$.

3.2. *The Seller*

Recall that the seller can make capacity commitments at a unit cost c_1 and make on-demand capacity enhancements at a higher unit cost c_2. The seller's cost function for serving customer θ (assuming he signed the contract), conditional on capacity ρ, and marginal costs c_1, c_2 for levels below ρ and above ρ respectively, is

$$C(\rho;\theta) = c_1\rho + \frac{c_2}{b(\theta)} \int_\rho^{b(\theta)} (q - \rho)dq \tag{7}$$

Given the type of the consumer (given θ), the seller minimizes the above function, obtaining

$$\rho^* = \beta_1 b(\theta) \tag{8}$$
$$C^*(\theta) = \beta_2 b(\theta) \tag{9}$$
$$\tag{10}$$

where

$$\beta_1 = \frac{c_2 - c_1}{c_2} \tag{11}$$
$$\beta_2 = \frac{c_1(c_2 - 0.5c_1)}{c_2}. \tag{12}$$

The seller's revenue function from serving type θ under the three-part tariff (F, Q, p) is

$$T(\theta) = \left(F + \frac{p}{b(\theta)} \int_{Q}^{b(\theta)} (q - Q)dq\right) \tag{13}$$

For the co-designed progressive mechanism where the buyer chooses Q (according to Eq. 4), the seller's revenue function simplifies to

$$T(\theta) = \alpha_2 b(\theta) \tag{14}$$

In all the above cases, the seller wants to choose prices and capacity (and, for the three-part tariff, Q) to maximize $T(\theta) - C(\rho; \theta)$, subject to the participation constrain $T(\theta) \leq V(\theta)$.

4. Discussion

In the simple, benchmark, case where there is only one type of buyer θ, and the seller has perfect information about buyer's type (so that the seller knows $b(\theta)$ and $V(\theta)$) it is easy to design an optimal three-part tariff. In fact, there are multiple solutions, in each of which the seller can extract full surplus. Some of these special solutions are

(1) $Q = b(\theta)$. Then $(V, b(\theta), p)$ is optimal for any p.
(2) $Q = 0, F = V$. Then $(V, 0, 0)$ is optimal, an "all you can eat" tariff with $p = 0$.
(3) $Q = 0, F = 0$. Linear tariff with $p = \frac{2V}{b}$ is optimal, and expected consumption $\frac{b}{2}$.

For the progressive co-designed tariff, also, the seller can optimally set any prices satisfying

$$\left\{\begin{array}{l} p_1 = p_2\left(1 - \sqrt{1 - \frac{2V(\theta)}{p_2 b(\theta)}}\right) \\ p_2 = \frac{bp_1^2}{2(b(\theta)p_1 - V(\theta))} \end{array}\right\}. \tag{15}$$

On the capacity side, the seller can find the optimal capacity

$$\rho^* = \frac{b(\theta)(c_2 - c_1)}{c_2} \tag{16}$$

as long as he knows, as we assumed here, the buyer's type θ.

Thus, when the seller has perfect information, the complex tariff structures provide no added gain relative to the simpler structures such as linear tariff and all-you-can-eat flat-rate. A type θ buyer evaluates a tariff

(F, P, Q) only in terms of total cost $R(\theta)$ and is indifferent to the tariff components as long as they keep total cost the same, hence the existence of multiple solutions to the problem. Moreover, comparing the three-part tariff with the incentive-compatible tariff structure, we see that when the seller knows $b(\theta)$ (alternately, $V(\theta)$) there is no advantage or loss in involving the buyer in mechanism design.

However this simple solution breaks down the moment there is either heterogeneity in buyer types or when there is a single buyer whose type θ is unknown to the seller. Now the seller faces additional problems in designing the optimal three-part tariff. First, while there are multiple tariffs that extract full surplus from the marginal customer $\hat{\theta}$, these tariffs will yield different revenues for $\theta > \hat{\theta}$. Thus, the seller not only has to make a price-volume tradeoff but also needs to determine how to set the tariff components. Secondly, in the face of demand uncertainty (but with a commitment to supply arbitrary capacity at a variable fee p) the seller has to determine how to contract for supply, given his own tradeoff between a precommitted capacity at lower unit cost and on-demand procurement at higher unit cost.

In this situation, we find that the co-designed progressive tariff makes an interesting contribution. By announcing (p_1, p_2) with $p_1 < p_2$ the seller not only gives the buyer an incentive to commit to some quantity, but also creates a mechanism for information revelation. That is, the buyer's choice of Q^* serves as a signal of the buyer's expected consumption, thus passing some private information from buyer to seller. The "cost" of this information, i.e., the information rent, is the revenue reduction to the seller due to the buyer's optimal choice of quantity at the lower price (the revenue aspect is a zero-sum game). Hence, a co-designed tariff presents a tradeoff to the seller, better capacity planning (hence lower costs) but potentially lower revenue. This tariff structure is therefore likely to be valuable when there is greater demand uncertainty and higher difference in costs between precommitted and on-demand capacity.

Our analysis also reveals an interesting relationship between the co-designed tariff and three-part tariffs. A (p_1, p_2) tariff is really a menu of three-part tariffs that share a certain property. That is, it is the same as a menu in which all components have the same variable fee for excessive use: $\{(p_1 Q_1, Q_1, p_2), (p_1 Q_2, Q_2, p_2), \dots (p_1 Q_k, Q_k, p_2)\}$. This is striking, given that in practice most firms that use three-part tariffs (e.g., wireless service providers) offer a menu of three-part tariffs (F_i, Q_i, p_i) where the p_i's are identical, and where higher F_i's are attached to higher Q_i's.

In conclusion, we note that the distinctive characteristics of a utility computing market—demand uncertainty, information asymmetry, and a dynamic supply chain—inspire a careful and deeper look at specialized price structures. The timing of the demand shock makes the usual approach to nonlinear pricing (menu of prices, with quantity discounts) less effective, because it forces the buyer to commit, with no recourse, without having full information about her demand. This sets the stage for the use of two-part or three-part tariffs, where the fixed fee provides a consumption commitment while the variable fee offers a recourse for additional capacity. But, three-part tariffs are extremely difficult to solve under information asymmetry and moreover do not reveal information about demand uncertainty. This indicates that industry should consider the role of co-designed tariffs with progressive variable prices, which not only help in information revelation but also offer an indirect way to announce a menu of three-part tariffs.

References

1. Anonymous. Survey: Computing power on tap. *The Economist*, 359(8227):16–20, June 23 2001.
2. A. Baratloo, P. Dasgupta, V. Karamcheti, and Z. M. Kedem. Metacomputing with MILAN. In *Proceedings of the 8th Heterogeneous Computing Workshop*, pages 169–183, April 1999.
3. R. Buyya, D. Abramson, J. Giddy, and H. Stockinger. Economic models for resource management and scheduling in grid computing. *Concurrency and Computation: Practice and Experience*, 14:1507–1542, 2002.
4. L. ChunLin and L. Layuan. A two level market model for resource allocation optimization in computational grid. In *CF '05: Proceedings of the 2nd conference on Computing frontiers*, pages 66–71, New York, NY, USA, 2005. ACM Press.
5. K. B. Clay, D. S. Sibley, and P. Srinagesh. Ex post vs. ex ante pricing: Optional calling plans and tapered tariffs. *Journal of Regulatory Economics*, 4(2):115–38, 1992. available at http://ideas.repec.org/a/kap/regeco/v4y1992i2p115-38.html.
6. E. Deelman, C. Kesselman, G. Mehta, L. Meshkat, L. Pearlman, K. Blackburn, P. Ehrens, A. Lazzarini, R. Williams, and S. Koranda. GriPhyN and LIGO, building a virtual data Grid for gravitational wave scientists. In *Proceedings of the 11th IEEE International Symposium on High Performance Distributed Computing*, pages 225–34, Piscataway, NJ, 2002. IEEE Computing Society.

7. I. Foster. The Grid: A new infrastructure for 21st century science. *Physics Today*, 55(2):42–47, 2002.
8. I. Foster and C. Kesselman. Globus: A metacomputing infrastructure toolkit. *The International Journal of Supercomputer Applications and High Performance Computing*, 11(2):115–128, Summer 1997.
9. I. Foster and C. Kesselman. The Globus project: A status report. *Future Generation Computer Systems*, 15(5–6):607–621, 1999.
10. I. Foster, C. Kesselman, and S. Tuecke. The anatomy of the Grid: Enabling scalable virtual organizations. *International Journal of Supercomputer Applications*, 15(3), 2001.
11. W. Hoschek, J. Jaen-Martinez, A. Samar, H. Stockinger, and K. Stockinger. Data management in an international Data Grid project. In *IEEE/ACM International Workshop on Grid Computing*, Bangalore, India, December 17-20 2000.
12. A. Lambrecht and B. Skiera. Paying too much and being happy about it: Existence, causes, and consequences of tariff-choice biases. *Journal of Marketing Research*, 2006. forthcoming.
13. U. M. Malmendier and S. Della Vigna. Overestimating self-control: Evidence from the health club industry. Technical report, Stanford Research Paper No. 1880, 2005.
14. K. W. Tse, W. K. Lam, and P. K. Lun. Reservation aware operating system for grid economy. *SIGOPS Oper. Syst. Rev.*, 37(3):36–42, 2003.
15. S. Venugopal, R. Buyya, and L. Winton. A grid service broker for scheduling distributed data-oriented applications on global grids. In *Proceedings of the 2nd workshop on Middleware for grid computing*, pages 75–80, New York, NY, USA, 2004. ACM Press.

PRICING SUBSTITUTABLE GRID RESOURCES USING COMMODITY MARKET MODELS

K. VANMECHELEN, G. STUER AND J. BROECKHOVE
Department of Mathematics and Computer Sciences
University of Antwerp
Middelheimlaan 1, Antwerp, Belgium
Email: kurt.vanmechelen@ua.ac.be

Enhancing Grid technology with market models for trading resources, is a promising step for Grids to become open systems that allow for user-centric service provisioning. This paper introduces a market model for trading substitutable Grid resources in a commodity market. We develop a pricing scheme and evaluate the market mechanisms through simulation. We show that the resource market achieves price stability and correctness, allocative efficiency and fairness.

1. Introduction

Through the virtualization and subsequent interconnection of computing infrastructure, Grid technology is steadily moving forward in realizing the vision of turning computing resources into a utility. Grids reinstate a computing model which is based on the use of a *shared* computing infrastructure. Unlike previous forms of this shared computing model, the infrastructure, as well as its user base, now span administrative and geographical boundaries. As a consequence, the issues of managing property and usage rights, and managing the infrastructure have become more complex. Property and usage rights management is crucial for Grids to become *open* systems in which the barriers for taking on a user or provider role are low, or non-existent. In order to lower these entry barriers, incentives have to be created for providers to join the computing infrastructure. In addition, users have to be encouraged to consume Grid resources in a well considered fashion. An important part of managing the infrastructure involves making allocation decisions such that the Grid's resources are used in an "optimal" way. Although system-centric approaches to this optimality have been predominantly used in the past, an alternative is to formulate the optimization problem from the user's perspective. Allocation decisions are then steered by the user's valuation of their results, instead of system-oriented metrics such as utilization and throughput. Such a user-centric form of service provisioning has the potential of delivering higher utility to the individual users of the system[1].

The introduction of a resource market is a promising step for dealing with both issues of openness and user-centric optimization. Firstly, connecting user valuations to a notion of *cost* and to a common unit of *currency*, results in an economically inspired model for making resource allocation decisions. This allows for a fine grained and uniform expression of potentially complex user valuations through prices, which is a key step in realizing the vision of user-centric Grid resource management. Secondly, if users are endowed with limited budgets and if providers are able to convert earned currency into a personal utility, we create the necessary incentives for entering Grids in a provider role, and for well considered resource usage by users. Presently, approaches exist that use a commodity market model for obtaining global equilibrium prices[2]. We extend these approaches with support for trading and pricing substitutable goods, and provide an evaluation of the market behaviour through simulation results.

2. Commodity Market model

This section describes the choices we have made in modelling our resource market. Modelling a resource market involves a choice on the types and units of the goods that will be traded in the market, as well as the behaviour of the market participants.

2.1. *Resource and job model*

In our current simulation setup, we have limited the types of computational resources to CPUs. Every provider hosts a number of CPU slots which represent a fixed share of the provider's computing infrastructure. In order to introduce price diversification on the speed of the provided CPU slots, we define `fast` and `slow` slot categories, thereby introducing two substitutable good types into the market model. As a consequence, consumers will be faced with the problem of deciding which of the two categories to buy for a particular job. This differs from the work presented in[2] wherein a commodity market model is set up with two complementary goods in the form of CPU slots and disk storage. The introduction of substitutable good types is important in the context of Grid markets, as it allows consumers to express their valuation of the properties a certain good type represents.

Indeed, although CPUs of comparable performance can be considered as interchangeable commodities, CPUs with distinct performance characteristics cannot. Performance can have a potentially large effect on the utility a CPU provides to a consumer, and should therefore be reflected in its price level. Consider for example, a consumer that can only adhere to a deadline requirement by allocating jobs to high performance CPUs.

We model jobs as CPU-bound computational tasks. Every job has a nominal running time T, expressed as the number of simulation steps it takes for the job to finish on a reference CPU slot r. When jobs are allocated to a CPU slot in category i, their actual running time is determined by $\frac{T}{PerfRatio_i}$ with $PerfRatio_i$ the performance ratio between CPU slot category i and r. Jobs are also taken to be atomic, in the sense that they are always allocated to a single CPU slot.

2.2. *Consumer model*

Consumers formulate demand in the market by expressing their willingness to buy CPU slots from providers in order to run their jobs. In every simulation step, consumers are charged with the usage prices for all Grid resources that are currently allocated to their jobs. The usage price for a particular resource is fixed at the market price level that was in place when the job was allocated to that resource. The consumers of our market are endowed with a limited budget which is periodically replenished according to a budget refresh period (the *allowance period*). Consumers do not attempt to save up credits but try to use up all of their budget, and expenditures are spread out evenly across the allowance period.

In every simulation step, consumers are faced with the problem of determining a demand vector on the resource types traded in the market. For the case under consideration here, this means that a consumer has to decide on the amount of `fast` and `slow` CPU slots it is willing to buy, given a price vector $\mathbf{p}$. We define a price vector $\mathbf{p}$ as $\mathbf{p} = (p_1, ..., p_n), p_i \geq 0$, where p_i represents the unit price of the ith commodity. Consumers show preference for a CPU slot type i according to Eq.(1). The lower the consumer's $Pref_i$ value, the higher the consumer values a CPU slot of type i.

$$Pref_i = P_i/(PerfRatio_i * PrefFactor_i) \tag{1}$$

with P_i the price for CPU slot type i, $PerfRatio_i$ the performance ratio of type i in relation to the reference CPU type r and $PrefFactor_i$ the personal preference factor a consumer assigns to type i. The preference factor is a simple abstraction for the complex logic a consumer might follow to prefer one CPU slot type over another outside of pure cost considerations. As an example, consider the situation wherein a consumer optimizes for total turnaround time and has a job graph which includes a critical path. Such a consumer would be willing to pay more for fast resources to be assigned to jobs on the critical path.

2.3. *Provider model*

Providers supply CPU resources to the computational market in the form of CPU slots. Every provider is configured with a fixed number of slots for each slot type present in the market. For a given price vector $\mathbf{p}$, providers have to determine their supply vector which is calculated according to Eq.(2).

$$Supply_i = FC_i * \min(1.0, \frac{P_i}{S_i}) \tag{2}$$

with FC_i the number of free CPU slots of type i, P_i the current price for type i, and S_i the average price for which the provider has sold slots of type i in the past. An elasticity attribute E determines the window for the average.

3. Pricing scheme

Prices can serve the role of a common bus to communicate complex consumer and provider valuations of goods and services. Market participants react to each other's valuations without knowing the details of how these come to be. This is important as it allows for a distributed form of value expression and a self-organizing way of controlling resource allocation in Grids. Furthermore, market participants are forced to react to price changes. Prices can force the market to a state in which consumers that value the use of Grid resources the most, are also able to allocate these resources. A prerequisite for all of the above points to have the desired effect however, is that price levels are set correctly and that the market is brought to equilibrium. In economic terms, this means that price levels for goods should be set in such a way that supply and demand for those goods are balanced out. According to Smale[3], such an equilibrium price point $\mathbf{p}^*$ exists so that $\xi(\mathbf{p}^*) = 0$ for any market that contains n interrelated commodities, with $\xi(\mathbf{p})$ the excess demand vector for price vector $\mathbf{p}$. Using D and S for the demand and supply functions of our market, the excess demand function ξ is given by $\xi(\mathbf{p}) = D(\mathbf{p}) - S(\mathbf{p})$. The components of the excess demand vector can be positive or negative, denoting overdemand or oversupply respectively.

For a market in which there are N types of tradable goods, we are faced with an N-dimensional optimization problem. In order to solve it, we have used an adaptation[4] of Smale's algorithm[5] as the basis for our iterative search algorithm. However, a number of issues arise in the practical application of this algorithm within our computational market. Firstly, if supply and demand are expressed as integral numbers, the reaction to a price change is not continuous and is not guaranteed to lead to a change in excess demand. In such a situation, we cannot determine a new direction for the search process. Therefore, the individual supply and demand functions of consumers and providers have been adjusted to return fractional values. In the aggregation of global demand and supply, we correct for the surplus of demand or supply generated this way. Secondly, our search process may strand on a *oversupply plateau.* An oversupply plateau is a part of the search space on which all prices result in zero demand and a uniform, non-zero supply. We introduce an artificial slope on these plateaus to steer the algorithm towards lower prices. Finally, we have to guard the search process from moving into the realm of negative prices, since Smale's algorithm does not enforce prices to be positive.

4. Evaluation

We have implemented the market model discussed in the previous sections in a discrete event simulator. In this section, we present an evaluation of the workings of our resource market. We focus on the following desirable market properties:

(1) Prices should be set in such a way that market equilibrium is reached.
(2) Price ratios for different goods should reflect the mean valuation ratios of those goods by the consumer population as a whole.
(3) The resource market should lead to fair allocations.
   (a) In an oversupply situation, every consumer should be able to acquire an equal share of the infrastructure if the job spawning rates for all consumers are equal.
   (b) In an overdemand scenario wherein consumers are not limited by a shortage of jobs in their queues, a consumer should be able to allocate a share of the total utility equal to its budget share.

(4) The measured resource utilization levels should be equal or close to the maximal achievable utilization level.
(5) Prices should be stable in the sense that limited, short-term changes in supply and demand lead to limited, short-term price responses.

In order to evaluate the fairness of our market, we introduce four consumer groups with distinct allowance levels. A consumer c in allowance group AG_i is allocated a budget $B_c = A * AF_i$ with A the base allowance for all consumers and AF_i the allowance factor for AG_i. We evaluate market fairness by establishing that the average budget share of consumers in AG_i equals their average infrastructural share.

In the absence of any real-world reference data for configuring our simulated market, we investigate aforementioned properties under two distinct and typical scenarios. The first scenario represents a market in *oversupply* which means that on average, the total available CPU time in the market is greater than the total computational time requested by all consumer jobs. Following[2] we inject a diurnal characteristic into the job flow in order to evaluate market efficiency and stability under sudden demand changes. The simulation parameters for the oversupply scenario are given in Table 1. The highest achievable utilization rate in this scenario is 63.3%.As shown in the graph in Fig.1, utilization levels start at 100% during the first job peak and slowly decrease as we move into oversupply. At the following job peak, the utilization levels rise again. The average utilization level for the infrastructure at the end of the simulation is 63.15%. Our market thus exhibits a high allocative efficiency, even in scenarios wherein our provider population strives for maximization of revenue instead of infrastructural utilization. This fulfills property 4.

Figure 1 also shows that our prices follow supply and demand closely. At the job induction steps, the prices of both goods are immediately adjusted to bring the market to equilibrium. After a price peak, prices decline as demand drops below the supply level due to a shortage of jobs and the market returns to the steady state in which there is oversupply. This indicates that prices are stable in the sense that price levels gradually return to their steady state, in the presence of shock effects introduced at the job induction steps. This fulfills property 5. As shown in Table 2, the median of the norm has a value of 0.64 with a 95th percentile of 5.8. The prices set by our pricing scheme thus approach the market equilibrium very closely, thereby fulfilling property 1. The graphs in Fig.2 show the effect of our price alterations on the excess demand levels. The grey graph displays the

Table 1. Simulation Parameters

Parameter	Value
Simulation steps	450
# Consumers	100
# Providers	50
# `fast` CPU slots per provider	{1,2,...,8}
# `slow` CPU slots per provider	{2,3,...,15}
E attribute for all providers	∞
`fast` vs `slow` performance ratio	2.0
$Pref_{\texttt{fast}}$	[1.0,2.0]
$Pref_{\texttt{slow}}$	1.0
AF_{1-4}	{1.0,1.5,2.0,2.5}
Job length	{2,3,...,10}
Allowance period	100
Base allowance	500,000
Job induction period	100
Jobs submitted at induction step	{1,2,...,200}
New job probability per step	10%

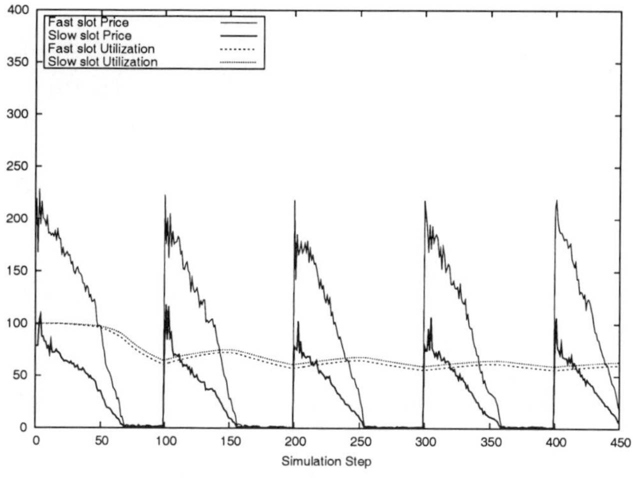

Figure 1. Price and utilization levels for `fast` and `slow` CPU slots in the oversupply scenario.

excess demand levels that would arise if we used the price calculated in step $i-1$, for step i. The black graph displays the excess demand levels for the prices calculated by our pricing scheme. We clearly see that the peaks in excess demand at the job induction steps are neutralized by our price adjustments.

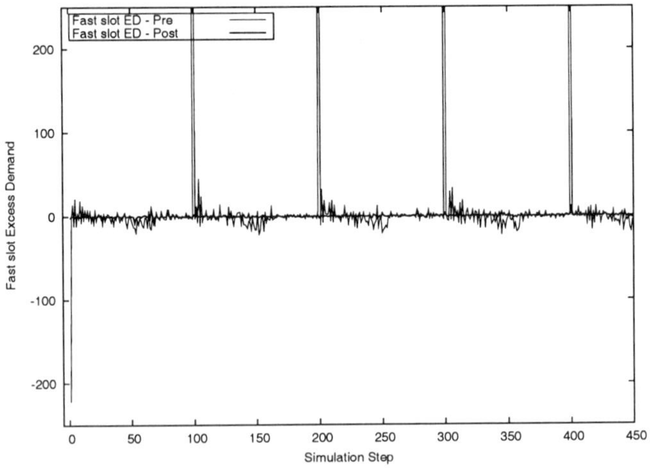

Figure 2. Excess demand levels in the oversupply scenario for `fast` CPU slots at step i for prices p_{i-1} and p_i

The mean preference factor for `fast` slots over the entire population is 1.5 and the performance factor is 2. Therefore, `fast` slots should be valued at three times the price of `slow` slots. Table 2 shows that price levels approximate this relative valuation, but are not in perfect correspondence with it. This can be explained by the fact that consumers favouring `fast` slots for a particular price vector, can still acquire `slow` slots with the budget they have left after buying their `fast` slots. The acquisition of these `slow` slots however, takes place regardless of their price. This elevates the aggregate demand for `slow` slots and their associated price level. If we disable this behaviour in the consumer strategy, the mean valuation factor is perfectly reflected in the price levels through a median price of 85.05 for `fast` slots and 28.13 for `slow` slots. Therefore we conclude that property 2 is fulfilled.

The graph in Fig. 3 shows the budget share and allocation share of the four consumer groups in the simulation. We notice that the allocation shares oscillate between the job induction pulses. This behaviour is to be expected; a consumer group with a high budget share is only able to allocate its affordable resource share fully when enough jobs are available in the consumer queues. As the job queues shrink, prices drop and other consumer groups are able to allocate resources. As prices converge to zero, the allocation shares remain approximately constant. When a new price peak arises, the allocation shares for wealthy consumers gradually rise again

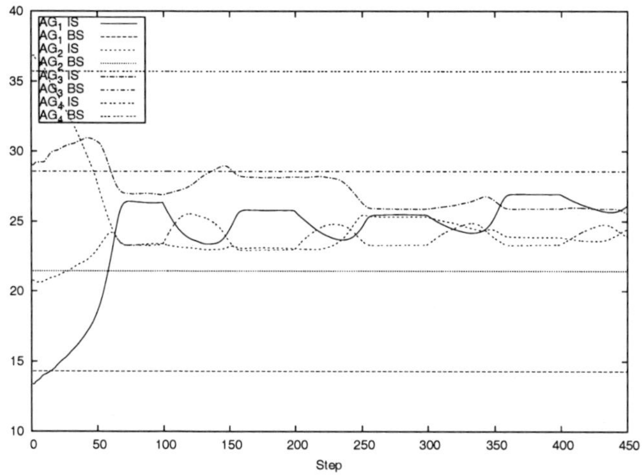

Figure 3. Mean budget and allocation shares per budget group for the oversupply scenario.

at the expense of the poorer consumers. The oscillatory effects are damped by the effect of averaging the allocation shares over all simulation steps. We see that allocation shares converge to the 25% mark. This corresponds with the notion that in a market with oversupply, differences in consumer budgets do not affect their allocation share in the long term, i.e. every consumer is able to allocate an equal share of the Grid's resources. This fulfills property 3a.

Our second scenario simulates a market in constant *overdemand*. The simulation parameters are the same as for the oversupply scenario, except for the fact that we keep the number of jobs in the consumer queues at a constant level. Although we do not present a detailed analysis here due to space considerations, all market properties are also fulfilled in the overdemand scenario, for which the results are also given in Table 2.

Table 2. Results from the oversupply and undersupply scenarios

	Oversupply Scenario	**Overdemand Scenario**
Median Norm	0.64	0.29
95th Percentile Norm	5.8	1.21
Median `fast` slot price	78.0	217.04
Median `slow` slot price	29.3	81.96
`fast` utilization	61.7%	99.6%
`slow` utilization	64.6%	99.7%
Maximal utilization	63.3%	100%

5. Future Work

A first aspect which needs further investigation is the ability of our system to deal with a higher dimensionality in the search space. This is important for extending our market model to more types of complementary, or substitutable goods. A second aspect of planned research is dealing with and modelling of resource locality, and the transport costs associated with it. A third aspect involves a study on the scalability of our approach. In particular, this includes an analysis on the network load introduced by our pricing scheme. Finally, we realize that for economically inspired resource sharing models to truly gain influence in contemporary Grid technology, we must transfer our ideas and techniques from a simulation environment to real-world environments.

6. Conclusion

Grid economies are a promising step in the development of open and user-centric Grid technologies. Through the introduction of resource markets in Grid resource management, the complexity of dealing with property and usage rights becomes manageable and fine grained user-centric service provisioning becomes possible. This work has presented a commodity market model for trading computational and substitutable Grid resources. The evaluation of our market model through simulation has shown that our market achieves the desirable properties of price correctness and stability, allocative efficiency and fairness.

References

1. B. N. Chun and D. E. Culler, "User-centric performance analysis of market-based cluster batch schedulers," in *CCGRID '02: Proceedings of the 2nd IEEE/ACM International Symposium on Cluster Computing and the Grid.* Washington, DC, USA: IEEE Computer Society, 2002, pp. 22–30.
2. R. Wolski, J. S. Plank, J. Brevik, and T. Bryan, "Analyzing market-based resource allocation strategies for the computational grid," *International Journal of High Performance Computing Applications*, vol. 15, no. 3, pp. 258–281, 2001.
3. S. Smale, "Dynamics in general equilibrium theory," *American Economic Review*, vol. 66, pp. 284–294, 1976.
4. M. Hirsch and S. Smale, "On algorithms for solving f (x) = 0," *Communications on Pure and Applied Mathematics*, vol. 32, pp. 218–312, 1979.
5. S. Smale, "A convergent process of price adjustment and global newton methods," *Journal of Mathematical Economics*, vol. 3, no. 2, pp. 107–120, 1976.

ARE UTILITY, PRICE, AND SATISFACTION BASED RESOURCE ALLOCATION MODELS SUITABLE FOR LARGE-SCALE DISTRIBUTED SYSTEMS?

XIN BAI, LADISLAU BÖLÖNI, AND DAN C. MARINESCU

School of Electrical Engineering and Computer Science
University of Central Florida
Orlando, FL 32816-2362, USA
Email: (xbai, lboloni, dcm)@cs.ucf.edu

HOWARD JAY SIEGEL

Department of Electrical and Computer Engineering
and Department of Computer Science
Colorado State University
Fort Collins, CO 80523-1373, USA
Email: HJ@ColoState.edu

ROSE A. DALEY AND I-JENG WANG

Applied Physics Laboratory
Johns Hopkins University
11100 Johns Hopkins Road Laurel, MD 20723-6099, USA
Email: (Rose.Daley, I-Jeng.Wang)@jhuapl.edu

In this paper, we discuss a resource allocation model that takes into account the utility of the resources for the consumers and the pricing structure imposed by the providers. We show how a satisfaction function can express the preferences of the consumer both regarding the utility and the price of the resources. In our model, the brokers are mediating among the selfish interests of the consumers and the providers, and societal interests, such as efficient resource utilization in the system. We report a simulation study on the performance of the model.

1. Introduction

Resource management in a large-scale distributed system poses serious challenges due to the scale of the system, the heterogeneity and inherent autonomy of resource providers, and the large number of consumers and the diversity of their needs. Individual resource providers are likely to have different resource management objectives and pricing structures. In this case, direct negotiation between resource providers and consumers is very inefficient. We need a broker to mediate access to resources from different providers. A broker is able to reconcile the selfish objectives of individual resource providers who want to maximize their revenues, with the selfish objectives of individual consumers who want to get the most possible utility at the lowest possible cost, and with some global, societal objectives, e.g., to maximize the utility of the system.

To formalize the objectives of the participants, we use: (i) a consumer *utility function*, $0 \leq u(r) \leq 1$, to represent the utility provided to an individual consumer, where r represents the amount of allocated resources; (ii) a provider *price function*, $p(r)$, imposed by an individual resource provider, and (iii) a consumer *satisfaction function*, $s(u(r), p(r))$, $0 \leq s \leq 1$, to quantify the level of satisfaction of an individual consumer that depends on both the provided utility and the paid price.

The consumer utility function could be a sigmoid[7]

$$u = u(r) = \frac{(r/\omega)^{\zeta}}{1 + (r/\omega)^{\zeta}}$$

where ζ and ω are constants provided by the consumer, $\zeta \geq 2$, and $\omega > 0$. Clearly, $0 \leq u(r) < 1$ and $u(\omega) = 1/2$.

The provider price could be a linear function of the amount of resources:

$$p = p(r) = \xi \cdot r$$

where ξ is the *unit price.*

A consumer satisfaction function takes into account both the utility provided to the consumer and the price paid. For a given utility, the satisfaction function should increase when the price decreases and, for a given price, the satisfaction function should increase when the utility increases. A candidate satisfaction function is[6]:

$$s(u, p) = 1 - e^{-\kappa \cdot u^{\mu} \cdot p^{-\epsilon}} \tag{1}$$

where κ, μ, and ϵ are appropriate positive constants.

Several systems, such as Nimrod/G[3], Rexec/Anemone[4], and SETI@home[5], use market based models for trading computational resources. In this paper, we consider a model where the allocation of resources is determined by their price, their utility to the consumer, and by the satisfaction of the consumer.

2. A Utility, Price, and Satisfaction Based Resource Allocation Model

Consider a system with n providers offering computing resources and m consumers. Call $\mathcal{R}$ the set of providers and $\mathcal{U}$ the set of consumers. Consider provider R_j, $1 \le j \le n$, and consumer U_i, $1 \le i \le m$, that could potentially use resources of that provider.

Let r_{ij} denote the resource of R_j allocated to consumer U_i and let u_{ij} denote its utility for consumer U_i. Let p_{ij} denote the price paid by U_i to provider R_j. Let t_{ij} denote the time U_i uses the resource provided by R_j. Let c_j denote the resource capacity of R_j, i.e., the amount of resources regulated by R_j.

The term "resource" here means a vector with components indicating the actual amount of each type of resource:

$$r_{ij} = (r_{ij}^1\ r_{ij}^2 \ldots r_{ij}^l)$$

where l is a positive integer and r_{ij}^k corresponds to the amount of resource of the k-th type. The structure of r_{ij} may reflect the rate of CPU cycles, the physical memory required by the application, the secondary storage, and so on.

The utility of resource of the k-th type provided by R_j for consumer U_i is a sigmoid:

$$u_{ij}^k = u(r_{ij}^k) = \frac{(r_{ij}^k/\omega_i^k)^{\zeta_i^k}}{1 + (r_{ij}^k/\omega_i^k)^{\zeta_i^k}}$$

where ζ_i^k and ω_i^k are constants provided by consumer U_i, $\zeta_i^k \ge 2$, and $\omega_i^k > 0$. Clearly, $0 < u(r_{ij}^k) < 1$ and $u(\omega_i^k) = 1/2$.

The overall utility of resources provided by R_j to U_i could be:

- the product over the set of resources provided by R_j, i.e., $u_{ij} = \prod_{k=1}^{l} u_{ij}^k$, or
- the weighted average over the set of resources provided by R_j, i.e., $u_{ij} = \frac{1}{l}\sum_{k=1}^{l} a_{ij}^k u_{ij}^k$, where a_{ij}^k values are provided by consumer U_i.

We consider a linear pricing scheme $p_{ij}^k = \xi_j^k \cdot r_{ij}^k$, though more sophisticated pricing structures are possible. Here ξ_j^k represents the unit price for resource of type k provided by provider R_j. The amount consumer U_i pays to provider R_j for a resource of type k is $p_{ij}^k \times t_{ij}$. The total cost for consumer U_i for resources provided by provider R_j is

$$p_{ij} = \sum_{k=1}^{l} p_{ij}^k \times t_{ij}$$

Based on Equation 1, we define the degree of satisfaction of U_i for a resource of the k-th type provided by provider R_j as

$$s_{ij}^k(u_{ij}^k, p_{ij}^k) = 1 - e^{-\kappa_i^k u_{ij}^k{}^{\mu_i^k} (p_{ij}^k/\phi_i^k)^{-\epsilon_i^k}}, \qquad \kappa_i^k, \phi_i^k, \mu_i^k, \epsilon_i^k > 0$$

where μ_i^k and ϵ_i^k control the sensitivity of s_{ij}^k to utility and price; ϕ_i^k and κ_i^k are normalization constants; ϕ_i^k is a reference price; and $\kappa_i^k = -\log\alpha$, with α a reference value for the satisfaction function. Detailed information about these parameters can be found in Bai.[1]

The overall satisfaction of consumer U_i for resources provided by R_j could be:

• the product over the set of resources provided by R_j, i.e., $s_{ij} = \prod_{k=1}^{l} s_{ij}^k$, or

• the weighted average over the set of resources provided by R_j, i.e., $s_{ij} = \frac{1}{l}\sum_{k=1}^{l} b_{ij}^k s_{ij}^k$, where b_{ij}^k values are provided by consumer U_i.

We consider a *provider-broker-consumer model* that involves a broker B. In this model, the amount of resources to be allocated is determined according to a *target utility* (denoted as τ), i.e., the broker allocates an amount of resources such that the utility of each type of resource to the consumer reaches this τ value. The broker also has "societal goals" and attempts to maximize the average utility and revenue, as opposed to providers and consumers that have individualistic goals. To reconcile the requirements of a consumer and the candidate providers, a broker chooses a subset of providers such that the satisfaction is above a threshold and all providers in the subset have equal chances to be chosen by the consumer. We call the size of this subset *satisficing size*, and denote it as σ. Detailed information about the model can be found in Bai et al.[2]

Several quantities are used to characterize the resource management policy for broker B and its associated providers and consumers:

• The average hourly revenue for providers. The revenue is the sum of revenues for all of its resource types. This average is over the set of all providers connected to broker B.

• The consumer admission ratio. This ratio is the number of admitted consumers over the number of all consumers connected to B. A consumer is admitted into the system when there is a provider able to allocate some of the resources requested by the consumer, otherwise the consumer is dropped.

• The average consumer overall utility. This average is over the set of all admitted consumers connected to broker B.

• The average consumer overall satisfaction. This average is over the set of all admitted consumers connected to broker B.

3. A Simulation Study

We simulate a system of 100 clusters and one broker. The number of nodes of these clusters is a random variable normally distributed with the mean of 50 and the standard deviation of 30. Each node is characterized by a resource vector containing the CPU rate, the amount of main memory, and the disk capacity. For example, the resource vector for a node with one 2 GHz CPU, 1 GB of memory, and a 40 GB disk is $(2GHz, 1GB, 40GB)$. Initially, there is no consumer in the system. Consumers arrive with an inter-arrival time exponentially distributed with the mean of 2 seconds.

The parameters of the utility function of consumers, i.e., u_{ij}^k, are uniformly distributed in the intervals shown in Table 1. The CPU rate, memory space, and disk space of a request, r_{ij}^k, are exponentially distributed with the mean of $2GHz$, $4GB$, and $80GB$, and in the range of $[0.1GHz, 100GHz]$, $[0.1GB, 200GB]$, and $[0.1GB, 1000GB]$, respectively.

Table 1. The parameters for the simulation are uniformly distributed in the intervals displayed in this table.

Parameter	CPU	Memory	Disk
ξ	[5, 10]	[5, 10]	[5, 10]
ω	[0.4, 0.9]	[0.5, 1.5]	[10, 30]
κ	[0.02, 0.04]	[0.02, 0.04]	[0.02, 0.04]
μ	[2, 4]	[2, 4]	[2, 4]
ϵ	[2, 4]	[2, 4]	[2, 4]
ϕ	[40, 60]	[80, 120]	[1800, 2200]

The *demand-capacity ratio* for a resource type k is the ratio of the amount of resources requested by the consumers to the total capacity of resource providers for resource type k, $\sum_j c_j^k$. In our model, the consumers do not provide the precise amount of resources needed, they only specify their utility function. In the computation of the demand-capacity ratio, for each consumer and each resource, it is assumed that for the requested r_{ij} value the corresponding u_{ij} value is 0.9. The *demand-capacity ratio* vector for all resource types is $\eta_j = (\eta_j^1\ \eta_j^2 \ldots \eta_j^l)$. To simplify the interpretation of the results of our simulation we only consider the case when $\eta_j^1 = \eta_j^2 = \cdots = \eta_j^l = \eta$. The service time t_{ij} is exponentially distributed with the mean of λ seconds. By varying the λ value we modify demand-capacity ratio so that we can study the behavior of the system under different loads.

For a multi-dimensional resource, we let the overall utility be the product of the utility of all types of resource, and we let the overall satisfaction be the product of the satisfaction of all types of resource.

We investigate the consumer admission ratio, the average hourly revenue, the average consumer satisfaction, and the average consumer utility for different target utility (Figures 1) and satisficing size (Figure 2) under various scenarios of demand-capacity ratio (Figures 3). We also compare the system performance of our scheme for several σ values with a *random strategy* where we randomly choose a provider from the set of all providers, without considering the satisfaction function. We study the evolution in time. In each case, we run the simulation 50 times and show the average value and a 95% confidence interval.

Figure 1 (a) shows that when $\tau = 0.8$, $\tau = 0.85$, and $\tau = 0.9$, the consumer admission ratio is approximately 1.0, and the three plots overlap with each other. When $\tau = 0.95$, during the transient period some consumer requests are dropped. As time goes on, the consumer admission ratio increases. More consumers can be admitted into the system due to the resource fragmentation[a]. In the steady state the admission ratio is 1. Figure 1 (b) shows that the average hourly revenue increases during the transient period, decreases due to the resource fragmentation, and then reaches a stable value. The larger is τ, the more resources are allocated to consumers, and the higher is the average hourly revenue. Figure 1 (c) shows that the average consumer satisfaction increases during the transient period and then reaches a stable value. The average consumer satisfaction is higher when τ is smaller; the smaller is τ, the more consumers can be admitted by resource providers with cheaper prices and these consumers experience higher satisfaction. Figure 1 (d) shows that the average consumer utility decreases during the transient period due to the resource fragmentation and then reaches a stable value. The average consumer utility is lower when τ is smaller.

Figure 2 (a) shows that the consumer admission ratio is approximately 1.0 for all cases. Figure 2 (b) shows that the average hourly revenue increases during the transient period, decreases due to resource fragmentation, and leads to a stable value. A small value of σ limits the number of choices the broker has and this restriction leads to lower average hourly revenues. The larger is σ, the higher is the average hourly provider revenue. The random strategy, which corresponds to the maximum value of $\sigma = \mid \mathcal{R} \mid$

[a]Resource fragmentation is an undesirable phenomena; in our environment the amount of resources available cannot meet the target utility value for any request and an insufficient amount of resources is allocated.

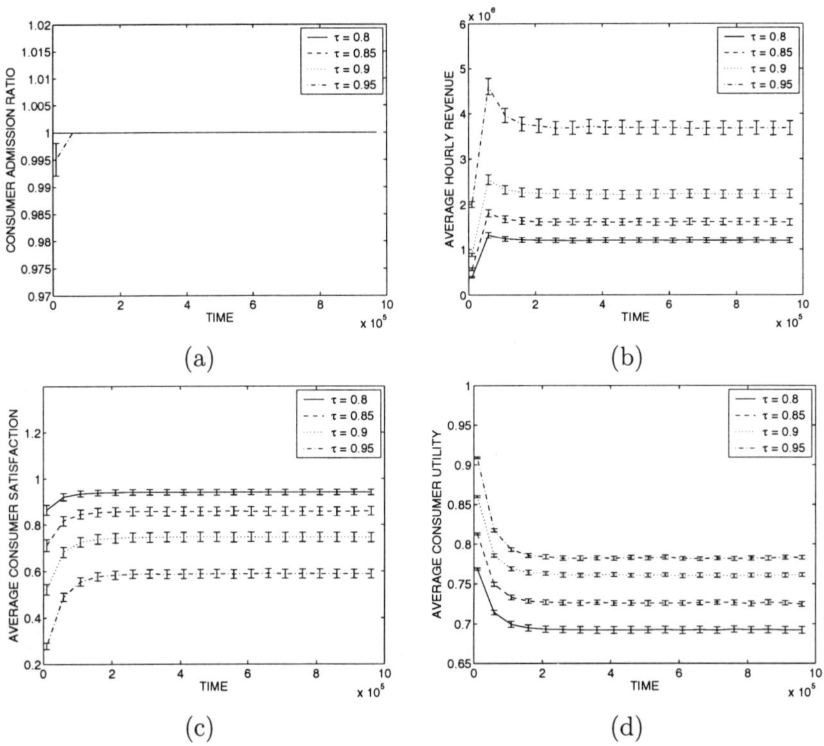

Figure 1. Consumer admission ratio (a), average hourly revenue (b), average consumer satisfaction (c), and average consumer utility (d) vs. time (in seconds) for $\sigma = 1$, $\eta = 1.0$, and $\tau = 0.8$, 0.85, 0.9, and 0.95.

has the highest average hourly provider revenue. Figure 2 (c) shows that the average consumer satisfaction increases during the transient period and then leads to a stable value. The average consumer satisfaction is higher when σ is smaller. Indeed, when $\sigma = 1$ we direct the consumer to that resource provider that best matches the request. When we select at random one provider from the set of all providers we observe the lowest average consumer satisfaction - we have a high probability to select a provider that is not with the highest satisfaction. Figure 2 (d) shows that the average consumer utility drops during the transient period due to the resource fragmentation and then reaches a stable value. The average consumer utility is lower when σ is smaller. The random strategy has the highest average consumer utility; when σ is larger consumers have a better chance to get resources according to the τ values.

Figure 3 (a) shows that when η is set to 0.25, 0.50, or 0.75, the system

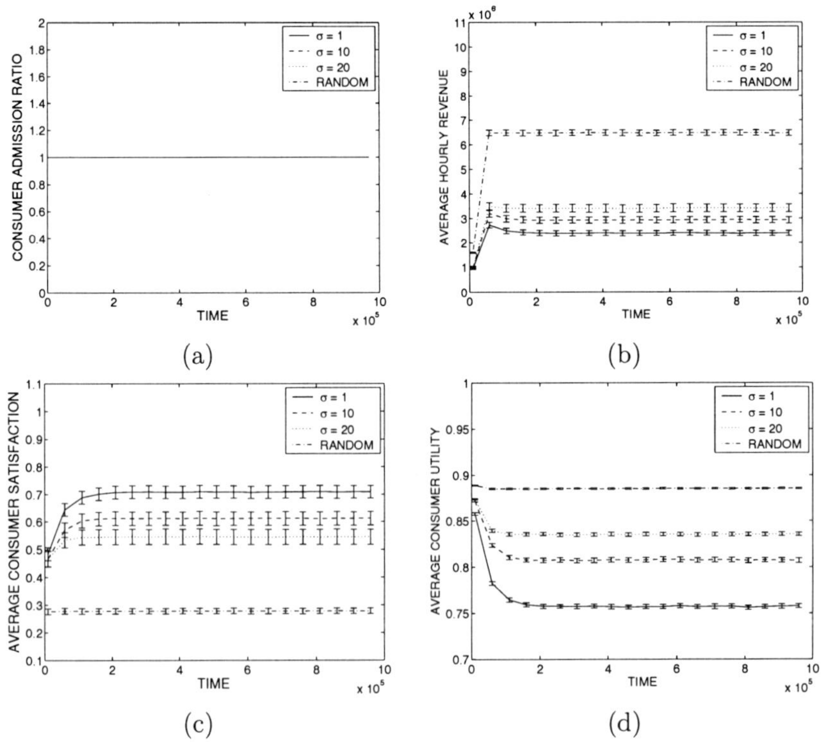

Figure 2. Consumer admission ratio (a), average hourly revenue (b), average consumer satisfaction (c), and average consumer utility (d) vs. time (in seconds) for $\tau = 0.9$, $\eta = 0.5$, and $\sigma = 1$, 10, and 20. For the random strategy, $\sigma = \mid \mathcal{R} \mid = 50$.

is capable of handling all requests and the corresponding plots overlap with each other. When $\eta = 1.0$ some requests are dropped. As time goes on, the consumer admission ratio increases due to resource fragmentation. During the steady state the consumer admission ratio is 1. Figure 3 (b) shows that the average hourly revenue increases during the transient period, and then decreases to reach a steady value. The larger is η, the higher is the average hourly revenue. The average consumer satisfaction drops during the transient period, increases due to resource fragmentation, and then converges to a steady value, as shown in Figure 3 (c). The smaller is η, the earlier the system reaches the steady state and the higher is the average consumer satisfaction. The average consumer utility drops during the transient period and then reaches a steady value, as shown in Figure 3 (d). The smaller is η, the earlier the system reaches the steady state and the higher is the average consumer utility.

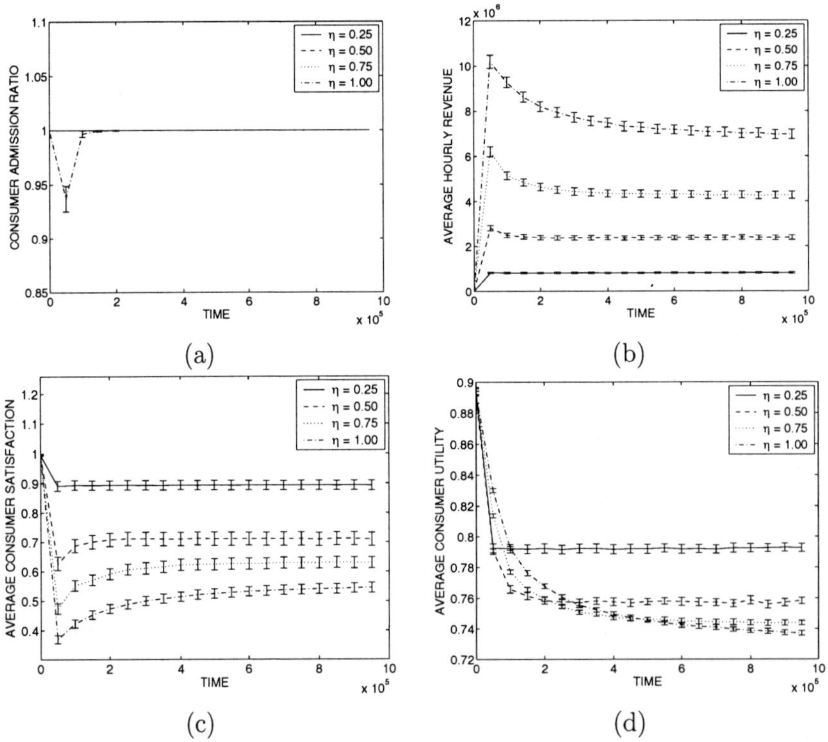

Figure 3. Consumer admission ratio (a), average hourly revenue (b), average consumer satisfaction (c), and average consumer utility (d) vs. time (in seconds) for $\tau = 0.9$ and $\sigma = 1$.

4. Conclusions

Economic models are notoriously difficult to study. The complexity of the utility, price, and satisfaction based models precludes analytical studies and in this paper we report on a simulation study. The goal of our simulation study is to validate our choice of utility, price, and satisfaction functions, to study the effect of the many parameters that characterize our model, and to get some feeling regarding the transient and the steady-state behavior of our models. We are primarily interested in qualitative rather than quantitative results, and we are interested in trends rather than actual numbers. It is too early to compare our model with other economic models proposed for resource allocation in distributed systems, but we are confident that a model that formalizes the selfish goals of consumers and providers, as well as societal goals, has a significant potential. This is a preliminary study that cannot provide a definite answer to the question posed in the title of the paper. Our intention is to draw the attention of the community to the potential of utility, price, and satisfaction based resource allocation models.

The function of a broker is to monitor the system and set τ and σ for optimal performance. For example, if the broker perceives that the average consumer utility is too low, it has two choices: increase τ or increase σ. At the same time, the system experiences an increase of average hourly revenue and a decrease of average consumer satisfaction. We note that while the utility is always increasing with the amount of allocated resources, the satisfaction also takes into account the price paid and exhibits an optimum at a certain level of resources. Increasing the resources beyond the optimum will still increase the utility but yield lower satisfaction, because the additional utility was paid an unjustifiably high price.

The simulation results shown in this paper are consistent with those in Bai et al.[2], where we use a much simpler model based upon a synthetic quantity to represent a vector of resources.

5. Acknowledgments

This research was supported in part by National Science Foundation grants MCB9527131, DBI0296035, ACI0296035, and EIA0296179, the Colorado State University George T. Abell Endowment, and the DARPA Information Exploitation Office under contract No. NBCHC030137.

References

1. X. Bai. *Coordination, Matchmaking, and Resource Allocation for Large-Scale Distributed Systems.* PhD thesis, University of Central Florida, 2006.
2. X. Bai, L. Bölöni, D. C. Marinescu, H. J. Siegel, R. A. Daley, and I.-J. Wang. A brokering framework for large-scale heterogeneous systems. *To be presented at the 15th Heterogeneous Computing Workshop*, Rhodes Island, Greece, April 2006.
3. R. Buyya, D. Abramson, and J. Giddy. Nimrod/g: An architecture of a resource management and scheduling system in a global computational grid. In *Proc. of the 4 th Int. Conf. on High Performance Computing in the AsiaPacific Region*, volume 1, pages 283–289, 2001.
4. B. Chun and D. Culler. Market-based proportional resource sharing for clusters. Technical report, University of California, Berkeley, September 1999.
5. SETI@home. URL http://setiathome.ssl.berkeley.edu/.
6. H. R. Varian. *Intermediate Microeconomics: A Modern Approach.* Norton, New York, March 1999.
7. M. Xiao, N. Shroff, and E.-P. Chong. Utility-based power control in cellular wireless systems. In *INFOCOM 2001, Joint Conf. of the IEEE Computer and Communication Societies*, pages 412–421, 2001.

Identity Economics & Anonymity of Distributed Systems

THE ANALYSIS FOR THE TRUST POLICY OF GRID SYSTEM BASED ON AGENT BASED VIRTUAL MARKET SIMULATION

Junseok Hwang, Choong Hee Lee, Ie-Jung Choi

Techno-Economics & Policy Program, Seoul National University, Seoul, Korea
{junhwang, lovethe2, matt00}@snu.ac.kr

So-young Kim

Korea Institute of Science and Technology Information, Daejeon, Korea
sykim8171@kisti.re.kr

The Grid Computing Technology is earning interest as the new generation of information and communication infrastructure which will replace the Internet. Presently, various countries all around the world are achieving the reduction of cost with the increment in capacity and quality through the commercialization of various grid services[1][2]. To construct and commercialize Grid services, the trustworthiness of the system is just as important as the technological advance and service profitability. On the basis of this observation, our research considers the system policy which is required to guarantee appropriate trust among system participants by modeling the Grid service market in a form of N personnel repeated prisoners' dilemma. As a result of the virtual market analysis it is shown that, when the system policy for trust is not implied properly, the Grid service market cannot attain sustainable growth. Especially, the effects of sharing level of the transaction information and restriction level of service usage nominal were evaluated in a various point of performance including total quantity of transaction, rate of cooperative transaction, and welfare. In conclusion, implications of appropriate policy alternatives are indicated on specific pursuits of the system to enable trust based Grid service market.

1. Introduction

The reputation and trust management in the internet including the E-commerce has been an important issue in both academic and industrial areas. The risk and uncertainty of E-commerce usually takes place when each consumer does not have enough information on the credit of the opposite trader. Akerlof(1970) had discussed the difficulty of trustful transaction in a market where information asymmetry exists between the buyers and sellers[3]. The seller has the exact information on the quality of the product and own transaction strategy, while the buyer has to make a 'good guess' on the product quality and seller's strategy with only restricted information. This situation has been studied and analyzed with the prisoners' dilemma of game theory. Axelrod(1984) showed that cooperative behaviors could be induced by iterative interactions among agents in his research on N personnel repeated prisoners' dilemma game. It's because the cooperative behavior will add positive information on one's reputation, causing higher return in the future, in a repeated game[4].

The research on trust has also been active in the computer science sector. Marsh(1994) established the trust model of each individuals as a numerical form in the distributed artificial intelligent community. He fixed the 'memory span' and 'cooperation threshold' variously, and displayed successful strategies among agents depending on the initiative conditions such as population distribution[5]. Since then, many researchers have studied to induce cooperation in the E-commerce[6], P2P[7][8] and Grid[9][10][11] environment, and the formation and evolution of trust in distributed environment which doesn't promise enough repeated transaction has also been studied[12]. Through former studies, trust management system based on the reputation have proved the potential of reducing the risk and uncertainty of transaction caused by asymmetric or incomplete information[13][14].

However, recently the researches focused on notifying probable dangers of trust management system are increasing with the mature of trust related technologies[15][16]. In this paper, we especially focus on the conflict between privacy protection and reputation transparency. In the following chapters, Grid service transaction market is computationally modeled and analyzed, and we try to present the direction of proper trust system policy based on this computational works considering information sharing level, identity restriction level and penalty level.

2. Prisoners' Dilemma of the Grid System

Table 1. Payoff Matrix of Grid Computing Service Transaction Market

		Supplier	
		Cooperation (C)	Denial (D)
Consumer	Cooperation (C)	*V+VA-P, P-V*	*-P, P*
	Denial (D)	*V+VA, -V*	*0,0*

V = Supplier's value of transacted computing service (*V>0*)

VA = Additionally created value through the utilization of transacted computing service by consumer (*VA>0*)

P = Price of transacted computing services in Grid Computing Service Market (*P>0*)

The transaction behavior between service user and resource providers in the Grid system can be described as the prisoners' dilemma of game theory[17]. Although the amount of total benefit is larger than any other situation when both service user and provider cooperate trustworthily, their choices in Nash equilibrium are the invasions of promised honors. This can be explained by table 1. In the given payoff matrix, denial behaviors are dominant strategies to both suppliers and consumers, since payoff from the denial has higher values to both of the parties. Accordingly, the Nash equilibrium of this prisoners' dilemma of Grid service market becomes the strategy set, (D,D).

However, the outcome of the game can be differentiated with the infinite repetition. In case of the infinitely repeated game, the payoff of current behavior can be calculated by the summation of present values of expectations. If all the participants of the Grid service market have strong tendency of reciprocal behaviors, we can assume that they will use the trigger strategy cooperating only when all the former behaviors of the opposite player were cooperative. Under this assumption, the present value of payoffs with cooperating and denying behaviors can be concretely calculated if we assume the value of discount rate(δ). As shown in equation (1) and (2), both will choose to cooperate in transactions when the expected benefit of cooperation is larger than that of the denial.

$$(V + VA - P) + \delta(V + VA - P) + \delta^2 (V + VA - P) + \Lambda > (V + VA) \qquad (1)$$

$$(P - V) + \delta(P - V) + \delta^2 (P - V) + \Lambda > P \qquad (2)$$

The equations above can be reorganized as the constraints for the discount rate. If the value of discount rate satisfies both the equations (3) and (4), the Grid market can sustain the trustworthiness of transaction among the consumers and suppliers who are assumed to use economically rational strategies in order to optimize self-interests.

$$\delta > \frac{P}{V + VA} \qquad (3)$$

$$\delta > \frac{V}{P} \qquad (4)$$

If the number of market participants is too large to transact with the same opposite repeatedly, the logic of repeated game may not be the proper explanation. However, if the market participants can share the historical information, they can use trigger strategy based on the shared information. Nowak and Sigmund called this kind of mechanism as indirect reciprocity, and they explained the shared historical information, 'image score,' as the reputation of the people[12]. In real markets, players who emphasize trust with transacting partners win the reputation among competitors, and the reputation induces benefit in the future. So, many people do not act as the myopic profit maximizer when trustworthy behavior generates less benefit presently. In this paper, we adopt the basic framework of prisoners' dilemma to make the agent-based model of the Grid service market with trust policy. In our model, agents have the chance to play the prisoners' dilemma repeatedly and they decide their strategies for the transaction based on the reputation information and the profitability of each behavior. In the following chapters, the payoff matrix, strategy decision process of each agent, and mainly considered trust policy of analyzed virtual market will be explained in detail.

3. Basic Assumptions for Agents' Payoff and Strategy Selection in Virtual Market

In our model, the payoff(U_T) generated by the Grid transaction is the same as table 1 and each agent gains additive payoff(U_P) as in the following equation.

$$U_i = U_T + U_P \tag{5}$$

U_T is determined by the payoffs of transaction, and U_P is determined by the trust policy. U_P is composed of three parts: the disutility from privacy invasion, the disutility from charged penalty about uncooperative behavior, and the utility from redistribution of gathered penalties. The invasion of privacy happens only when the agents' transacting behaviors are recorded, therefore the disutility from the privacy invasion is assumed to occur only when the agents are monitored to form their reputation. The Equation (6) shows the expected payoff, $E(U_P)$, depending on trust policy. P_M is the probability of monitoring, and P_D is the probability of uncooperative transaction.

$$\begin{aligned} E(U_P) &= P_M(-U(privacy\_value)) + P_M P_D(-U(penalty\_value)) \\ &+U(re-distributed\_system\_income\_from\_penalties) \end{aligned} \tag{6}$$

In the simulation of this paper, we assumed the value of P, V and VA as 1, 1 and 0.5 to calculate U_T. The reduction of payoff originated from privacy invasion is assumed to have the value, 0.1, in the case of sensitive users on privacy invasion and the value, 0.02, in the case of insensitive users.

All the agents in virtual market are designed as the profit maximizers adapting their strategies based on the historical information of each strategy. They are encoded to consider the transition of their strategies by comparing the expected payoffs of each behavior when they achieve losses more than twice continuously, and possibility of changing their strategies increases as the transition produces benefit larger compared to the maintenance of it. Additionally, to guarantee the individual rationality condition on participating in transactions, agents are assumed to leave the market when their accumulated payoff cannot fulfill minimum requirements, and agents authorize transacting partners who have larger reputation value than the individually required minimum reputation†). Lastly, the size of newcomers to the virtual market is assumed to be proportional to the aggregated payoff of all the participating agents.

4. Explanation for the Simulated Trust Policy Alternatives

Level of information sharing, identity restriction and punishment, which were applied as parameters to change the trust policy in this paper, are combined as below and formed into Grid service transaction market with heterogeneous attributes.

Table 2. Setting of Policy Parameters in Each Trust Policy Alternative

Policy Alternatives	Level of Information Sharing and Punishment		Identity Restriction
P1	Max	Strong Punishment	Max
P2	Max	Weak Punishment	Max
P3	Max	Strong Punishment	Mid
P4	Max	Weak Punishment	Mid
P5	Max	Strong Punishment	Min
P6	Max	Weak Punishment	Min
P7	Mid	Strong Punishment	Max
P8	Mid	Weak Punishment	Max
P9	Mid	Strong Punishment	Mid
P10	Mid	Weak Punishment	Mid
P11	Mid	Strong Punishment	Min
P12	Mid	Weak Punishment	Min
P13	Min	No Punishment	Max
P14	Min	No Punishment	Mid
P15	Min	No Punishment	Min

† Marsh(1994) in his work categorized agents as optimist, realist and pessimist depending on the level of difficulties in giving credit to decide the cooperation. He assumed that each agent has heterogeneous tendency in setting the minimum value as 'cooperation threshold[5].'

Policy Alternatives from P1 to P5 enforces the maximum sharing of recorded information. Furthermore, the recorded information is always provided to the requesting users. Under the Policy Alternatives from P7 to P12, the level of information sharing is medium, and this is encoded by recording the half of transactions randomly. For Policy Alternatives from P13 to P15, none of the information is shared.

The Policy Alternatives from P1 to P12 were modeled to punish users presenting non cooperative behavior. The punishment levels are divided into strong and weak punishment. The strong punishment is defined to be redemption of all the profit made by non cooperative behavior, and the weak punishment is defined to be redemption of half the profit. Additionally, because the record and the distribution of personal information by the system cause the privacy invasion, the personal value, which each user gave to privacy protection, was subtracted from the benefit of a transaction when information is shared.

Identity restriction level is maximum in Policy Alternatives P1, P2, P7, P8, P13 where once a user participates in the market, the identity is unchangeable and when reentering the market, the former transaction records are continued. In Policy Alternatives P3, P4, P9, P10, P14 the level of identity restriction is medium and here a new identity can be created with a certain cost. This cost is imposed by the non cooperative strategy toward newly generated identity during the initiative period of the simulation [18]. Lastly, for Policy Alternatives P5, P6, P11, P12, P15, the identity restriction level is lowest and the participants can change their identity whenever they want. In these alternatives, it is expected that users intentionally act uncooperatively and reenter the market with a new identity after cleaning the trust level record[8][*)].

5. Simulation Results depending on Trust Policy Alternative Adoption

As introduced in chapters above, the changes of information sharing level and identity restriction alters the profit distribution, depending on the behavioral strategies. So, the specific alternative of trust policy can vary the amount of transaction and cooperation. The fitness of a policy alternative could be judged by the aggregated response of the market according to policies. In this paper, to evaluate the appropriateness of the combined policies through the market reaction, following values resulted from the computational simulation were used.

1. Total transaction quantity: A1
2. Rate of inter cooperative transaction among completed transactions: A2

[*] In the former study of Feldman, this strategy is introduced with the name of 'White Wash,'

3. Sum of total individual users' profit: A3

Three categories of the aggregated market response in the simulation are all repeatedly calculated with two different values of the disutility from privacy invasion. In our simulation, number of agents in initiative status of the market is assumed as 1600, and agents are encoded to have 50% possibility of taking a role of seller and buyer in every period. In addition, all the buyer and seller agents are randomly matched, and transact cooperatively only when satisfied with cooperative threshold. The following examines the result of values A1, A2 and A3 in the virtual transaction market, with formerly explained 15 combined trust policies.

5.1. *Total Amount of Transactions*

It means the number of successful transaction unrelated to inter cooperativeness of transacting agents. Therefore, it could be used to show the effect of the trust policy on the quantitative growth of the market.

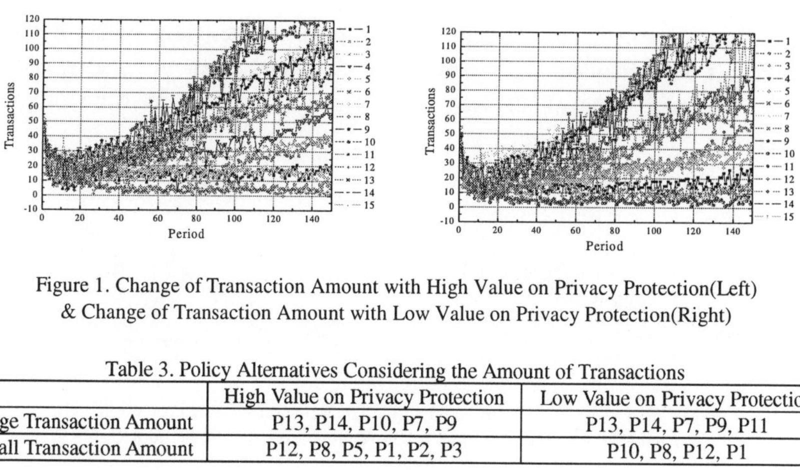

Figure 1. Change of Transaction Amount with High Value on Privacy Protection(Left) & Change of Transaction Amount with Low Value on Privacy Protection(Right)

Table 3. Policy Alternatives Considering the Amount of Transactions

	High Value on Privacy Protection	Low Value on Privacy Protection
Large Transaction Amount	P13, P14, P10, P7, P9	P13, P14, P7, P9, P11
Small Transaction Amount	P12, P8, P5, P1, P2, P3	P10, P8, P12, P1

5.2. *Rate of Cooperative Transactions*

Even though the amount of transaction and the number of participants are large, the quality of the system is not guaranteed if the rate of trustful transaction is not high. So, if the amount of transaction is the standard for the evaluation of quantitative perspective, the rate of cooperative transaction could be referred as the standard for the qualitative evaluation.

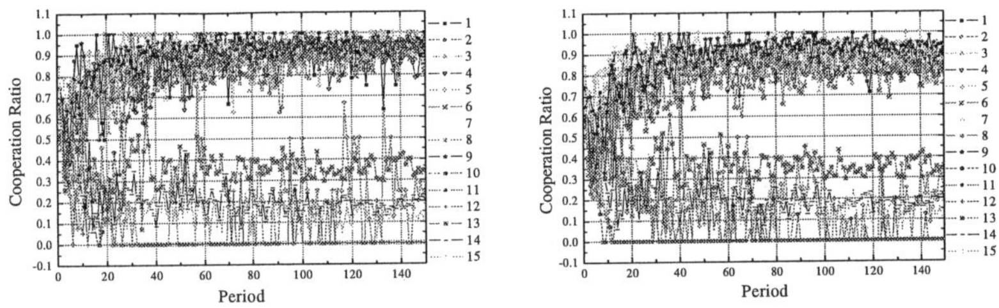

Figure 2. Rate of Cooperative Transactions with High Value on Privacy Protection(Left) & Rate of Cooperative Transactions with Low Value on Privacy Protection(Right)

Table 4. Policy Alternatives Considering the Rate of Cooperative Transactions

	High Value on Privacy Protection	Low Value on Privacy Protection
High Cooperativeness	P8, P12, P13, P14, P15	P8, P10, P12, P13, P14, P15
Low Cooperativeness	P1, P2, P3, P4, P5, P6, P7, P9, P10, P11	P1, P2, P3, P4, P5, P6, P7, P9, P11

5.3. *Social Welfare*

In our research, social welfare is defined in the view point of the J. Bentham's utilitarianism. We treated every individual's benefit equally, and the simply summed value of all users' payoff is used for the measure of social welfare

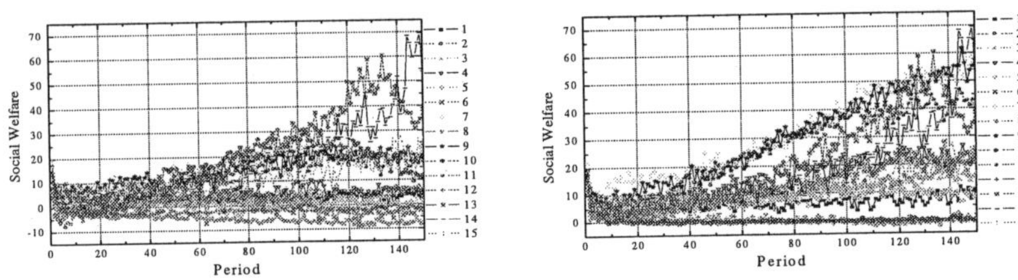

Figure 3. Changes of Welfare Level with High Value on Privacy Protection(Left) & Changes of Welfare Level with Low Value on Privacy Protection(Right)

Table 5. Policy Alternatives Considering the Changes of Welfare Level

	High Value on Privacy Protection	Low Value on Privacy Protection
High Welfare Level	P13, P14	P13, P14, P7, P9, P11
Medium Welfare Level	P15, P9, P11, P10, P7	P4, P6, P2, P3, P15
Low Welfare Level	P1,P2, P3, P4, P5, P6, P8, P12	P1, P5, P8, P10, P12

6. Conclusion and Discussion

Summing up the simulation results, we can extract three major guidelines which are helpful to construct trust policy of Grid system.

First, in expansion of the market, the increment of participants and transaction amounts is the most important pursuit of the system. Therefore, the decrement of information sharing is proper direction of trust policy. Second, to increase cooperative transactions in the market, we need to increase the level of information sharing, and also need to consider the increment of identity binding level. Third, to begin considering the social welfare, we should investigate the concerned level of privacy invasion. In our research, we assumed that the concerning about privacy invasion causes the reduction of payoff and the monitoring for the record of historical behaviors induces the concerns of privacy invasion.

In real Grid system, there can be more various negative impacts originated from trust policy related with accounting, authorizing and authenticating process. Accordingly, before the implementation of trust policy, we should consider all the feasible ways of lessening users' privacy concerns and risks through both the technologies and institutions. In our simulation, six trust policy alternatives of full information sharing with low penalty and medium information sharing with high penalty show similar superiority comparing to other alternatives when agents gain low disutility from monitoring. However, with the assumption of agents' higher sensitivity of privacy invasion, the increase in value of policy parameters related with information sharing and identity binding decreases social welfare. This is why the users who emphasize privacy protection want to reduce the surveillance and record. Consequently, they can be thought as assenting to the partial loss of cooperative transaction caused by loose trust policy.

In conclusion, the design for the trust policy of Grid market should consider the priority of pursuit such as the expansion of market size, the increment of transparent transaction and the protection of users' privacy. These pursuits of system can be maximized by the combination of specific system policies, but the difficulty occurs from the fact that one specific policy mix cannot generally maximize all the pursuits. In accordance with this fact, we should rank the priority of our purposes in trust policy formation before we design and implement it. If we want to enlarge the amount of market transaction to secure critical mass, the low level of information sharing and identity binding will be proper. However, if we need to increase the trustworthiness and transparency of market, we should take the opposite direction in setting policy mix. Lastly, if we want to optimize aggregated payoff of all the market participants, we need to balance the level of monitoring, information sharing, identity binding, and penalizing with the consideration of users' advantage from truthful market and disadvantage from surveillance.

The results in our research may not be applied to the design of Grid market trust policy directly because the assumptions of agents and virtual market do not reflect the real world entirely. However, it shows the special characteristics of trust policy originated from the tension between privacy protection and market transparency. Most of the former virtual market studies were centered on the efficiency and performance depending on market mechanism and architecture, but we need to satisfy all the requirements which are critical to the users. Trustworthiness and privacy protection are representative critical requirements in future Grid systems, and we need to advance our understanding about these areas. On the basis of this perspective, we anticipate that our research and its succession can be one of the building blocks in Grid system policy research.

References

1. I. Foster and C. Kesselman, The Grid: Blueprint for a New computing Infrastructure, Morgan Kaufmann Publishers Inc., 1998.
2. I. Foster, C. Kesselman and S. Tuecke, "The Anatomy of the Grid," International Journal of Supercomputer Applications, 2001.
3. G. A. Akerlof, "The market for "Lemons": Quality Uncertainty and the Market Mechanism," The Quarterly Journal of Economics, Vol. 84, 1970
4. R. Axelrod, The Evolution of Cooperation, Basic Books, 1984.
5. S. Marsh, "Formalising Trust as a Computational concept," Ph.D. Thesis, University of Stirling, 1994.
6. P. Resnick, K. Kuwabara, R. Zeckhauser and E. Friedman," Reputation systems," Communications of ACM, Vol.43, 2000
7. S. D. Kamvar, M. T. Schlosser and H. Garcia-Molina, "The EigenTrust Algorithm for Reputation Management in P2P Networks," Proceedings of 12th International World Wide Web Conference, 2003.
8. M. Feldman, K. Lai, I. Stoica and J. Chuang, "Robust Incentive Techniques for Peer-to-Peer Networks," Proceedings of the 5th ACM conference on Electronic commerce, 2004
9. F. Azzedin and M. Muthucumaru, "Towards trust-aware resource management in grid computing systems," In Proceeding of First IEEE International Workshop on Security and Grid Computing, 2002
10. F. Azzedin and M. Maheswaran, "A trust Brokering System and Its Application to Resource Management in Public Resource Grids," Proceeding of 18th International Parallel and Distributed Processing Symposium, 2004
11. B. Alunkal, I. Veljkovic and G. von Laszewski, "Reputation-based Grid Resource Selection," Argonne National Laboratory, 2003
12. M. A. Nowak and K. Sigmund, "Evolution of indirect reciprocity by image scoring," Nature, Vol.393, 1998
13. D. M. Kreps and R. Wilson, "Reputation and Imperfect Information," Journal of Economic Theory, vol. 27, 1982
14. P. Resnick and R. Zeckhauser, "Trust Among Strangers in Internet Transactions: Empirical Analysis of eBay's Reputation System," Working Paper for the NBER Workshop on Empirical Studies of Electronic Commerce, 2000.

15. G. Guerra, D. Zizzo, W. Dutton and M.Peltu, "Economics of Trust in the Information Economy: Issues of Identity, Privacy and Security," Oxford Internet Institute, University of Oxford Working Paper, 2003.
16. D. Gambetta, Trust: Making and Breaking Cooperative Relations, Basil Blackwell Inc., 1988
17. J. Hwang, C. Lee and S. Kim, "Trust Embedded Grid System for the Harmonization of Practical Requirements," Proceedings of IEEE International Conference on Service Computing, Vol.1, 2005
18. E. Friedman and P. Resnick, "The social cost of cheap pseudonyms," Journal of Economics and Management Strategy, Vol.10, 2000
19. H. Varian, Microeconomic Analysis 3rd edition, W.W. Norton, 1992
20. M. Weiss, "Models of Grid : Cost and Standard Implications," Proceedings of 1st IEEE International Workshop on Grid Economic and Business Models, 2004

Suggestions for Grid Commercialization Strategies

PRIVATE TO PUBLIC GRIDS

RICHARD CROUCHER
Sun Microsystems
USA

Sun Microsystems is leading the world with the first public Grid service offering, where any user with a valid credit card can submit jobs. Richard will talk about the challenges faced in offering this and the underlying trust continuum which has required Sun to develop its own multi-tenancy capabilities in order to support users with differing security and privacy concerns. These enable a single Grid infrastructure to be securely partitioned and allocated to users or organizations for which a public Grid offering is not currently acceptable.

BIODATA

Richard Croucher is a Technical Director with Sun Microsystems. He is currently the Chief Architect for Sun's Commercial Grid Computing Utility. He has been with Sun Microsystems for over 10 years and was formerly the Chief Architect of Sun's Professional Services team in EMEA; the largest UNIX system integration practice in Europe; where for the last few years he specialized on Data Centre Infrastructures and led the team which developed the Sun DCRA and DCRI. He is recognized as a thought leader within Sun's technical community and is part of the worldwide team architecting Sun's next generation of Grid products.

Prior to Sun, Richard worked at Amdahl Corporation for 6 years where he helped deploy UNIX on S/390 compatible Mainframes, establishing some of the first large scale, UNIX based Data Centers and co-existing with MVS. He has over 20 years of continuous experience with UNIX and has been in the IT industry for around 22 years. He started his career in the Research Laboratories at EMI, working as part of the team that developed the first Computer Tomography X-Ray Scanners.

He received diplomas in Applied Physics (1975), Electronics (1976) and a post degree qualification in the Non-Destructive Testing of Materials (1978). He was elected to membership of the British Computer Society in 1993. He is a Chartered IT Practitioner and a member of the BCS Elite club.

EGG: AN EXTENSIBLE AND ECONOMICS-INSPIRED OPEN GRID COMPUTING PLATFORM

J.BRUNELLE[*], P.HURST[‡], J.HUTH[‡], L.KANG[†], C.NG[†], D.C.PARKES[†], M.SELTZER[†], J.SHANK[‡] and S.YOUSSEF[§]

[*]*Department of Physics, Boston University, Boston, USA*
[†]*DEAS, Harvard University, Cambridge, USA*
[‡]*Department of Physics, Harvard University, Cambridge USA*
[§]*Center for Computational Science, Boston University, Boston, USA*

The *Egg* project provides a vision and implementation of how heterogeneous computational requirements will be supported within a single grid and a compelling reason to explain why computational grids will thrive. Environment computing, which allows a user to specify properties that a compute environment must satisfy in order to support the user's computation, provides a how. Economic principles, allowing resource owners, users, and other stakeholders to make value and policy statements, provides a why. The Egg project introduces a language for defining software environments (*egg shell*), a general type for grid objects (the *cache*), and a currency (the *egg*). The Egg platform resembles an economically driven Internet-wide Unix system with egg shell playing the role of a scripting language and caches playing the role of a global file system, including an initial collection of devices.

1. Introduction

Although grid software and its conceptual framework have evolved substantially in recent years, today's grids are still limited in size to hundreds of sites and thousands of computers. They have not approached Internet-scale. Grids have not grown larger and are not used more broadly due to five factors: 1) There is no global resource allocation mechanism. 2) Installing and maintaining grid infrastructure software is time-intensive and difficult. 3) Converting applications to be grid-enabled is also time-intensive and difficult. 4) It is complex to express user and organizational policies. 5) It is difficult, often impossible for users to express needs.

Grid computing will become mainstream only when its existence can be largely ignored. For example: when researchers can focus solely on computational experiments and not on the tools, configurations, and gaming of the system required to obtain sufficient resources, grid computing will be more popular. Similarly, when two organizations can share resources in a flexible and locally managed manner, those organizations are more likely to work together and share those resources.

We introduce *Egg*, a system that provides nearly transparent and natural access to grid resources. The Egg architecture brings together environment computing and economic principles to create a vision of grid computing that realizes the promise of autonomy and openness.

2. Egg Overview

Egg is an extensible, economics-based platform for open grid computing. Egg addresses the shortcomings of the existing grid solutions by focusing on the following design principles:

(1) **Simplicity and Extensibility**: Every grid function, for example, submitting jobs to run, storing files, assigning user permissions, should involve only a small set of standard operations, such as *put* and *get*.
(2) **Smart Resource Allocation**: Users can describe their jobs well in a language of computational experiments, but not in terms of characteristics of the machines that can run those jobs. Transparent resource discovery and allocation that are in the best interests of the users simplify interactions.
(3) **Decentralized Policy and Control**: All stakeholders must have a flexible and easily comprehensible way of influencing the overall system. Organizations with different resources can share resources by creating realistic economies while still retaining as much control as desired over policy.

All three principles are critical and are interrelated. Individually, each represents a significant breakthrough in the respective problem domain in grid computing. The three major components of Egg correspond to these principles: *egg shells* and *caches*, *microeconomic architecture*, and *macroeconomic architecture*. We discuss each in detail.

3. Fundamental Architecture

3.1. *Egg shells*

Egg shell is a language that allows a user to specify both the environment requirements, to be established via installation, together with the details of the computational job. This is the essential element of what we term *environment computing.* The details provided by a user can include information such as the location of source data and the name and location of the analysis program that is to be executed.

In fact, the inspiration for egg shell comes from the humble activity of installing software.[1] Egg shell is a small superset of the Pacman language, which is fast becoming the *de facto* standard for deployment of software environments on grids in the US research community. The Open Science Grid (OSG)[2] is entirely deployed with Pacman[3], as is the Virtual Data Kit, including installation of Condor and Globus and other grid middleware[4], as is ATLAS[5] and other experiments.[6]

There is one key egg shell primitive. This primitive, `put`, is used to add one type of cache to another type of cache and can be thought of as a generalized copy. For instance, `put` initiates a job, downloads and uploads data, or installs a software environment. Other egg shell primitives, such as `pay` can be defined in terms of `put`. The `pay` primitive initiates payment for a service rendered, and is defined as a `put` of egg currency (the *egg*) to a bank cache. The following example egg shell demonstrates the simplicity and expressivity of egg shell.

```
1: { put ~Alice/jobs/runningEnvironment.eggshell mygrid OR fail
         "Can't run on this machine." }
2: put ~Alice/jobs/binary1 mygrid
3: FOR j in [job1.eggshell,job2.eggshell,job3.eggshell] {
4:         put ~Alice/jobs/j mygrid
5:         put results/j.out ~Alice/results
6:         pay @100.Harvard.Alice when gmTime < 1-Apr-2006
7: }
8: shell echo "done"
```

Currency is denoted with `@` as a prefix, e.g. `@20.Harvard.Alice` denotes 20 units of Harvard currency held by Alice. Notice the conciseness of egg shell. In just 8 lines, it captures the configuration of the environment (line 1), dispatching jobs to machines (line 4), and payment terms (line 6).

---

[1] Pacman web site: (http://physics.bu.edu/pacman/).

[2] `www.opensciencegrid.org`

[3] See: `http://kb.grid.iu.edu/data/aths.html`

[4] `http://vdt.cs.wisc.edu/`

[5] The ATLAS project is a massive collaborative effort in particle physics, involving over 1800 physicists from more than 150 universities and laboratories in 34 countries. `http://atlas.web.cern.ch/Atlas/index.html`

[6] `http://atlas.bu.edu/caches/registry/E/htmls/registry.html`

A great deal of complexity and autonomy underlies the simplicity of egg shell. Line 1 (`put Alice/jobs/runningEnvironment.eggshell`) refers to a typical installation script.[7] Line 4 (`put Alice/jobs/j mygrid`) runs a job, without requiring that the user specify machines on which to run it or any characteristics about the job. The characteristics of the job are determined by agents local to caches, that learn these characteristics by observing the characteristics of past jobs. The payment terms in line 6 (pay @100.Harvard.Alice) provide all the guidance needed for the system to determine the best machine for the job, and indeed predict whether the job can be completed by the deadline.

3.2. *Caches*

All functional elements of Egg are *caches* including computers of various kinds, storage devices, bidding agents, files, directories, egg shell source and object files, banks, marketplaces, rolodexes printers, garbage cans etc. A cache can be thought of as a box with an input port that supports an operation of *put*-ing one cache into another. Caches have internal existence as python objects in the Egg system and an external existence as bindings to URLs or servers. The relationship that a cache has to the external world is maintained by a pair of functions *eval/save* which are generalizations of *read/write* combining i/o, search operations, lazy evaluation and individual cache-specific computations. For example, if an egg shell is *put* into a computer cache, the *save* operation may attempt to execute the egg shell. The same egg shell put into a bidding cache might, on the other hand, cause a bid to be constructed; a banking cache might strip the egg shell of currency and a storage cache might simply store the egg shell as a file.

4. Microeconomic Architecture

In Egg, we provide *smart resource allocation* via a microeconomic architecture, whereby caches compete with each other for the right to execute a job submitted by a user, described in egg shell. Egg manages the bidding process and determines a winner. In the short-term, the auction process provides a dynamic and robust resource allocation mechanism with prices

[7] For reference, a typical ATLAS installation consists of 1233 Pacman scripts such as the one above, with 20687 lines of egg shell in total and deploys about 4GB of software. Most of the ATLAS egg shells are produced automatically from their build system. Parts, however, are hand written. Pacman typically creates more than 1000 new installations per day around the world, with more than 800,000 downloads of Pacman to more than 50 countries as of March 12, 2006.

linked to resource demand. In the long term, prices provide signals to guide future investment in resources and allow for accounting by parties such as funding agencies. All local schedulers and bidding algorithms employed by caches are fully extensible to allow for continual improvement.

The first element in the microeconomic architecture is a *bidding language* that allows a user to state a willingness-to-pay. Egg does not require a user to state resource requirements explicitly. For example, a Physicist interested in running computational analysis on a local grid does not need to estimate the length of time, or file space, that the computational process requires. The responsibility for resource estimation is pushed to caches: a cache needs an estimate of resource requirements to determine its opportunity cost for accepting a job.

Egg supports an expressive language to allow users to describe a trade-off between completion time and value. A user can bid a *price schedule*, i.e. a willingness-to-pay for different job completion times. For simplicity we initially support a linear price schedule. For example, a typical bid defines (`@10.Harvard.Alice,@2.Harvard.Alice,Apr-01-06 00:00:01`), which describes a monotonically decreasing willingness-to-pay of $2 + (10 - 2)(t - t_0)/(t_d - t_0)$ eggs, where t is the time of completion, t_d is the maximal deadline (`Apr-01-06 00:00:01` in the example), and t_0 is the time at which the bid is submitted to Egg. A simple special case is a constant willingness-to-pay with a hard deadline. The bid is the *maximal* willingness-to-pay, the payment actually made by a user depends on the current balance of supply and demand. A user can also specify a *minimal reliability*, e.g. "I will only consider caches with reliability $\geq$ 99.9%." The Egg infrastructure maintains a *reliability* metric for caches, which is a measure of the frequency with which a cache has failed to meet a deadline.

Jobs are submitted (as egg shell) to multiple caches that satisfy the environment and reliability requirements specified in a job, and are willing to accept the currency specified by the user. Caches providing discovery services can facilitate this process of matching jobs with caches that are willing and able to generate bids. The job is ultimately allocated to the cache that responds with the lowest offer, and the cache receives this amount upon the successful completion of the job (and receives no payment otherwise.)

The microeconomic architecture carefully constrains this bidding process to provide *strategyproofness* to users: Egg guarantees that a user minimizes her payment and maximizes her chances of successful completion of the job if and only if she truthfully reports her willingness-to-pay and deadline considerations. Strategyproofness provides simplicity: Egg provides the benefits of an economic framework while hiding the potential complexities from users.

In achieving strategyproofness, while respecting the autonomy of caches, the most important architectural element is provided by *price tables*. Each cache represents its bid for jobs by populating entries in a price table. Loosely, a price table for cache i specifies a price $p_i(Q,t)$ for some quantity of resources Q allocated starting at time t. Egg requires monotonicity properties of prices in a price table, such that prices increase with larger quantities. Each cache must maintain prices up until a time horizon, some T time steps into the future. A cache can change entries in the price table, but can only *increase* its posted price $p_i(Q,t)$ for each (Q,t) pair. The Egg platform receives an estimate of compute resources $\hat{Q}$ from the cache, and then determines the bid from each cache by inspection of the price tables.

Caches retain flexibility to decide which kinds of jobs to schedule. For example, economically-motivated caches would set prices to maximize revenue given local knowledge about job characteristics and hardware characteristics.

5. Macroeconomic Architecture

The macroeconomic architecture in Egg is designed to support basic economic functions: the creation of currency, the security of currency, and currency exchange. Critically, and perhaps uniquely amongst current virtual economies, the Egg macroeconomy allows multiple currencies. This provides for complete autonomy with respect to policy to the many stakeholders on heterogeneous grids. Policy is then supported through the following mechanisms: (a) anyone can create a currency, "print" arbitrary quantities of the currency, and decide how to allocate currency to users; (b) an owner of compute or file servers can control access via restrictions on currency and identity, and by placing currency-specific limits on resource allocations.

Of course, just printing currency cannot make a user rich: currency only has value if it can be spent at caches, or exchanged for other currencies with spending power. On the other hand, anyone can be an Alan Greenspan (Bernard Bernanke?!) for their own economy. Every currency requires a bank, which is responsible for maintaining the security of the account of any user holding the currency, and also to provide important services such currency exchange. Moreover, every user has her own bank (even if she does not generate her own currency). These banks are involved in the transfer of currency between users.

Egg provides a secure identity infrastructure. For instance, the Harvard bank can certify its identity by the use of cryptographic signatures. When currency changes hands it is signed to indicate the parties involved in the exchange. For example, if Harvard generates 10 eggs and gives them to Laura then Laura's bank holds `@10.Harvard.Laura` eggs, indicating this transfer. The Harvard bank also keeps a record that Laura has 10 Harvard eggs. Laura can now grant `@5.Harvard.Laura` eggs to Saul and Saul's bank would hold `@5.Harvard.Laura.Saul` eggs. Saul's bank could also contact the Harvard bank, as the "bank of record" for Harvard eggs, and claim possession of these eggs at which point the Harvard bank would update its record.[8]

In Egg, caches can control access by specifying which currencies are accepted. For example, consider a simple computer cache which attempts to execute any egg shell given to it. If the cache accepts `@*.Saul` this is just as secure as putting Saul's public key in `.ssh/authorized_keys` (since Egg uses OpenSSL cryptography) with the substantial additional merit of having accounting, a chain of authorization if "*" is not the empty list, and a chance to pre-examine and record whatever Saul executes on the system. Similarly, if the computer accepts `@Harvard.*`, anyone holding Harvard currency can compute. In a more restrictive configuration with the computer accepting `@Harvard.Laura.?`, anyone who Laura gives Harvard currency to directly has access to the computer.

Caches which earn currency and which bid on incoming jobs will usually also have a *home currency* used as the unit of resource estimation and bidding. In such cases, the cache may earn accepted foreign currencies by using a bank to establish and exchange rate with the home currency.

In the global economy, it is partly through the control of monetary supply that countries can implement socio-economic policy and the same is true for the Egg economy. By allowing multiple currencies, a computational grid created by the Chinese government can interoperate with a computational grid created by the US government, but without either party ceding control of policy. China does not need to worry that the US bank will flood the economy with a surfeit of US eggs because users in China can hold China

[8]Thus, the Egg currency is not formally a bearer currency in the sense that a recipient bank cannot *independently* establish that the validity of eggs. But, we achieve good decentralization in practice, e.g. for transfers between mutually trusted banks. If Saul's bank is concerned about the security of Laura's bank (e.g. perhaps Laura's bank also gave 10 eggs to Margo), then in performing this transaction Saul's bank can first check with Harvard's bank that the eggs are still Laura's to transfer.

eggs, and the exchange rate would move against the US currency.

In a globe-spanning physics research project like ATLAS, the Egg platform would allow physicists to effectively allocate globally available resources directly in the natural terms of the research. Suppose that a high level policy decision concludes that analysis searching for the Higgs boson over the next month is so important that it requires 70% of the global ATLAS resources. The Egg currency allows a policymaker to specify this without making decisions on details such as who has access to which computers, storage and network resources, and with what priorities for what periods of time. By further delegation, someone managing the Higgs analysis effort can then provide additional refinement, e.g. specifying the fraction of resources are used for Monte Carlo simulation compared with analysis, or which persons or groups get to spend the currency. At the same time, owners of resources can maintain complete control over who has access to their systems and whether they contribute to the Higgs effort within ATLAS.

Note that the macroeconomic functions described here do not enter into consideration of the actors in the system. Users can organize resources that they have access to and can express their intentions in the currency units that they are familiar with when necessary.[9] Cache owners will simply list which currencies are accepted. Managers of organizations generate and transfer the currency that they are used to depending on needs and priorities.

Banks, like everything else in Egg, are also caches and autonomous agents in their own right and able to pursue local policies in establishing exchange rates. We intend to perform simulations to better understand the effect of various methods to compute exchange rates and perform exchange, both to understand robustness to shocks and also to determine which monetary metrics need to be instrumented by the Egg platform (e.g. real currency supply, inflation, etc.).

6. Closing Comments

Egg provides an extensible and economics-inspired open grid computing platform. This is a multi-year effort involving close collaboration between

[9] A user with `@BU` (Boston University) eggs can still state willingness-to-pay in BU eggs. Banks are used to generate quotes for currency exchange and enable competition across domains. Suppose a Harvard cache wins. On successful completion of the job, the Harvard bank would perform currency exchange from `@BU` into `@Harvard` eggs, credit these to the Harvard cache, and finally debit `@BU` eggs from the user's account. The net effect is that the Harvard bank is holding some `@BU` eggs.

computer scientists, computational physicists, and economists. Egg is spawning many subprojects. For instance: (a) statistical machine learning to predict resource requirements; (b) methods of computational mechanism design for sequential and strategyproof resource allocation; (c) opportunity-cost based schedulers; (d) algorithms to compute exchange rates; (e) languages for environment computing. Vital to Egg's success as a platform is its extensibility and openness: our current focus is on defining and implementing the Egg platform together with initial versions of various caches that we find useful. Continual innovation will ultimately provide for sustainable and successful grid computing.

6.1. *Related work*

The Globus Toolkit[10] and Condor [12] provide the current *de facto* architecture for resource management in grid computing. However, as argued by Foster et al. [9], grid computing is "brawn" without "brain." We'd go further and argue that grid computing is just too cumbersome and complex, and with insufficient kinds of expressiveness (for both policy and use), to approach Internet scale. Also, while Foster et al. [9] suggest the use of agent technology for the automatic creation of "virtual organizations" [6], our view is that stakeholders– funding agencies, Deans of engineering schools, managers, etc. –should be provided with mechanisms to implement policy while agents put to use to price resources, predict job characteristics, adjust exchange rates, and other such well-defined tasks. Dumitrescu et al. [5] provide an alternate vision of policy for computational grids.

Many papers have proposed using market-based methods for resource allocation in networked computing [2,11,15,8,16,14], some of which has focused specifically on computational grids and federated systems [13,1,18,17,10]. However, the combined microeconomic and macroeconomic architecture, coupled with attention to policy and the need for decision autonomy differentiates Egg from these earlier works. To give a couple of examples, we are not aware of any work that allows for multiple currencies and considers macroeconomic issues such as exchange rates, nor are we area of any work that provides for strategyproofness to users (i.e. non-manipulability) despite the dynamics of grid computing environments and while still supporting seller autonomy in setting local price policies.

The microeconomic architecture adopted in Egg is inspired by recent

[10]http://www.globus.org

theories on the design of strategyproof allocation mechanisms in dynamic environments [7]. The macroeconomic design shares some of the goals expressed in the work of Irwin et al. [4], for instance in recognizing the importance that currency schemes support policy and allow delegation of resource access rights. Clark et al. [3] have written at length about the success of the Internet as a network platform, especially about the role of openness and end-to-end arguments in the support of continual innovation.

Acknowledgments

This work is partially supported by NSF ITR 0427348.

References

1. R. Buyya, D. Abramson, , and J. Giddy. NimrodG: An architecture of a resource management and scheduling system in a global computational grid. In *In Proceedings of the 4th International Conference on High Performance Computing in Asia-Pacific Region*, pages 283–289, May 2000.
2. Brent N. Chun, Philip Buonadonna, Alvin AuYoung, Chaki Ng, David C. Parkes, Jeffrey Shneidman, Alex C. Snoeren, and Amin Vahdat. Mirage: A microeconomic resource allocation system for sensornet testbeds. In *Proceedings of 2nd IEEE Workshop on Embedded Networked Sensors (EmNetsII)*, 2005.
3. David D. Clark, John Wroclawski, Karen R. Sollins, and Robert Braden. Tussle in cyberspace: Defining tomorrow's Internet. In *Proc. ACM SIGCOMM*, 2002.
4. D.Irwin, J.Chase, L.Grit, and A.Yumerefendi. Self-recharging virtual currency. In *Workshop on Economics of Peer-to-Peer Systems*, 2005.
5. Catalin L. Dumitrescu, Michael Wilde, and Ian Foster. A model for usage policy-based resource allocation in grids. In *In PolicyWorkshop2k5*, 2005.
6. I. Foster, C. Kesselman, and S. Tuecke. The anatomy of the grid: Enabling scalable virtual organizations. *International Journal of SuperComputer Applications*, 15(3), 2001.
7. Mohammad T. Hajiaghayi, Robert Kleinberg, Mohammad Mahdian, and David C. Parkes. Online auctions with re-usable goods. In *Proc. ACM Conf. on Electronic Commerce*, pages 165–174, 2005.
8. I.E.Sutherland. A futures market in computer time. *Communications of the ACM*, 11:449–451, 1968.
9. I.Foster, N.R.Jennings, and C.Kesselman. Brain meets brawn: Why grid and agents need each other. In *Proc. 3rd Int. Conf. on Auton. Agents and Multi-Agent Systems (AAMAS)*, 2004.
10. K. Czajkowski and I. Foster and C. Kesselman and N. Karonis and S. Martin and W. Smith and and S. Tuecke. A resource management architecture for metacomputing systems. In *Workshop on Job Scheduling Strategies for Parallel Processing*, 1998.

11. K. Lai, B. Huberman, and L. Fine. Tycoon: A distributed market-based resource allocation system. Technical Report cs.DC/0404013, Hewlett Packard, 2005.
12. M. Litzkow, M. Livny, , and M. Mutka. Condor - A Hunter of Idle Workstations. In *Proceedings of the 8th International Conference of Distributed Computing Systems*, pages 104–111, June 1988.
13. M.Balazinska, H.Balakrishnan, and M.Stonebraker. Contract-based load management in federated distributed systems. In *First Symp. on Networked Systems Design and Impl. (NSDI)*, 2004.
14. I. Stoica, H. Abdel-Wahab, and A. Pothen. A microeconomic scheduler for parallel computers. In *Proceedings of the Workshop on Job Scheduling Strategies for Parallel Processing*, pages 200–218. Springer-Verlag, 1995.
15. M Stonebraker, R Devine, M Kornacker, W Litwin, A Pfeffer, A Sah, and C Staelin. An economic paradigm for query processing and data migration in Mariposa. In *Proc. 3rd Int. Conf. on Parallel and Distributed Information Systems*, pages 58–67, 1994.
16. Carl A Waldspurger, Tad Hogg, Bernado Huberman, Jeffrey O Kephart, and W. Scott Stornetta. Spawn: A distributed computational economy. *IEEE Trans. on Software Engineering*, 18:103–117, 1992.
17. R. Wolski, J. Brevik, J. Plank, , and T. Bryan. Grid resource allocation and control using computational economies. In *In Grid Computing: Making the Global Infrastructure a Reality*, pages 747–772. Wiley and Sons, 2003.
18. R. Wolski, J. Plank, J. Brevik, and T. Bryan. Analyzing market-based resource allocation strategies for the computational grid. *The International Journal of High Performance Computing Applications*, pages 258–281, 2001.

GRIDASP TOOLKIT*: AN TOOLKIT FOR GRID UTILITY COMPUTING

HIROTAKA OGAWA,
SATOSHI ITOH,
TETSUYA SONODA,
SATOSHI SEKIGUCHI

Grid Technology Research Center, AIST
Akihabara Dai Bldg, 1-18-13 Sotokanda,
Chiyoda-ku, Tokyo 101-0021, Japan

One of the biggest evolutions brought by Grid technology is "Grid Utility Computing", which utilizes various kinds of IT resources and applications across multiple organizations and enterprises, and integrates them into a comprehensive and valuable service. Since 2004, we proposed and have been developing the GridASP framework which realizes Grid-enabled Application Service Providers (ASP) so as to realize Grid Utility Computing. GridASP can bind Application Providers, Resource Providers, and Service Providers all together and provide application execution services with security and anonymousness to enterprise/scientific users. In this paper, we report the conceptual idea of GridASP and the detail of the framework now being developed. Information on GridASP can be found on www.gridasp.org.

1. Introduction

One of the biggest evolutions brought by Grid technology is "Grid Utility Computing", which utilizes various kinds of IT resources and applications across multiple organizations and enterprises, and integrates them into a comprehensive and valuable service.

Since 2004, we have proposed and been developing the GridASP framework which realizes Grid-enabled Application Service Providers (ASP) in order to realize Grid Utility Computing. GridASP mainly targets to technical enterprise applications such as Life sciences, Automotive, CAE, etc. And its major aims are:

- Improvement of ROI (Return On Investment) by teaming diverse specializations.
- Assisting start-up of new businesses by taking advantage of professional know-how.

* Web page: http://www.gridasp.org/

- Availability of a full range of feature-rich Application Services with no downtime.

To achieve these aims, GridASP can bind Application Providers, Resource Providers, and Service Providers all together and provide application execution services with security and anonymousness to enterprise/scientific users.

In this paper, we report the conceptual idea of GridASP and the detail of the framework now being developed.

2. Conceptual Model

First, we show the basic conceptual business model of GridASP framework which realizes grid-enabled Application Service Providers (see Figure 1.). GridASP consists of the following 3 different roles of entities.

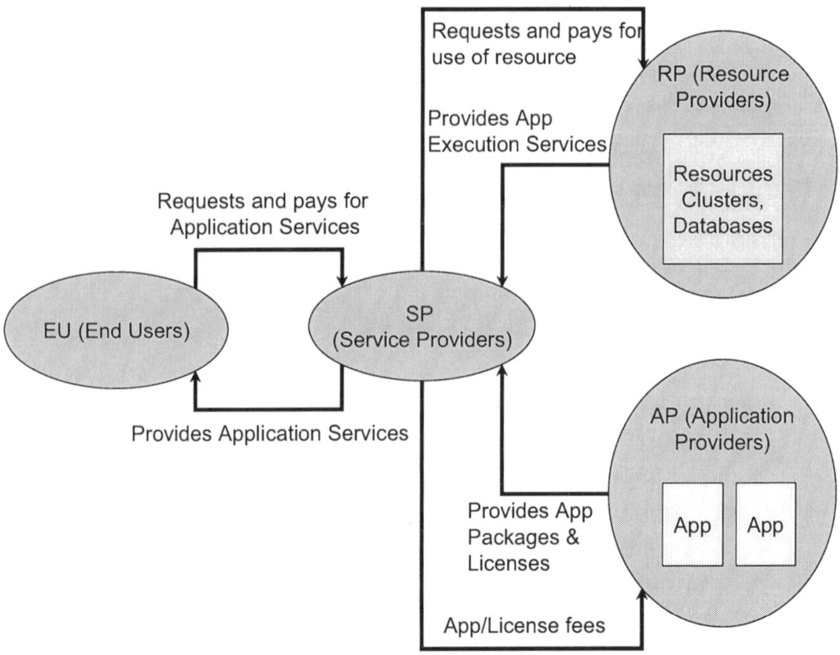

Figure 1 Conceptual Model of GridASP

1. Application Provider (AP)
   Application Provider is an entity of providing application packages and licenses and receiving application license fees from Service Provider (SP), based on the number of application deployment or usage.

2. Resource Provider (RP)
   Resource Provider is an entity of providing CPU and/or Storage resources and receiving fees from Service Provider (SP), based on the amount of resource usage or the cost of making use of their resources.
3. Service Provider (SP)
   Service Provider is an entity of integrating applications and IT resources into a comprehensive service and servicing it to end users, typically as a Web-based Grid portal service. SP charges fees on end users per use basis, and pays Application Providers and Resource Providers if need be.

Thanking to GridASP model, we believe, collaboration between these 3 entities can be enforced. It means, users can use value-added technical applications at lower cost, resource holders such as commercial data centers or computer centers can utilize their resources much more, and application vendors can obtain both of extra license fees and future enterprise and/or scientific customers.

3. GridASP Toolkit

Based on the conceptual model, we have been developing GridASP Toolkit which includes a portal construction toolkit and subsidiary tools. Figure 2 describes the architectural overview of GridASP Toolkit.

As well as several other portal toolkits such as GridPort Toolkit[1] and GridSphere[2], our portal toolkit is built on top of the current Grid and WWW (de facto) standard technologies, such as Jetspeed-1 portal framework[3], Globus Toolkit 3 and 4[4], and CoG kits[5]. And GridASP Toolkit provides a collection of services, scripts and tools to realize a general-purpose (non application specific) Grid portals, including user and authentication management, file/data management, job management, visualized workflow-job editor, resource brokering, and etc. Via our portal-based Web interface, users can submit their jobs into the underlying multiple clusters managed by LSF, Sun Grid Engine, and PBS.

GridASP is an open architecture that is designed to be capable of using other Grid services and technologies as they become available. And it is intended to provide a framework that resource holders and application vendors can build and join "Grid Utility Computing Business" based on the GridASP model, described as in Section 1.

As well as full-fledged Grid portal features, our portal framework also provides several GridASP-specific features. For brevity, we will briefly explain these features.

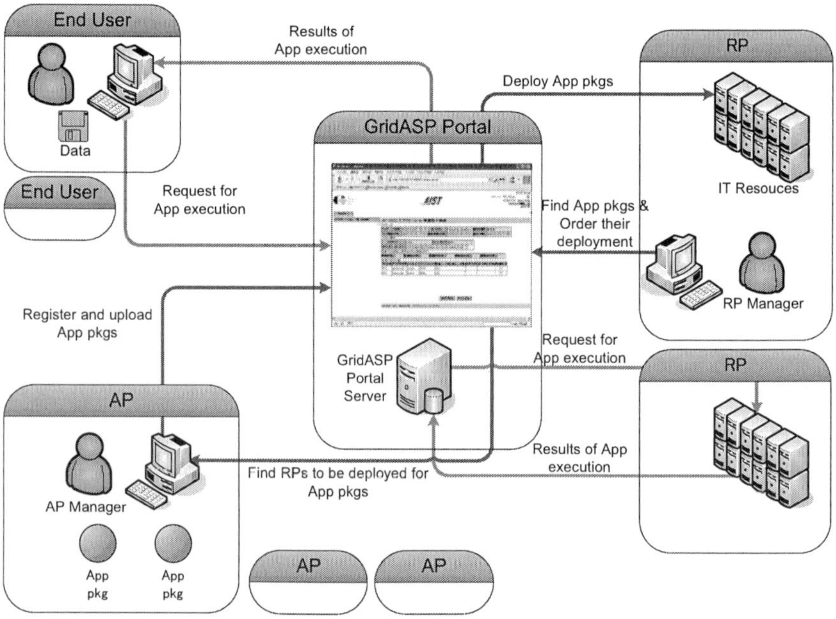

Figure 2 Architectural Overview of GridASP Toolkit

3.1. *Centralized Application/Resource Management*

GridASP portal provides Web-based interface not only for job execution but also for application and resource management (see Figure 3). Basically application and resource management requires several approval processes between APs, RPs, and SPs. For example, prior to deployment, RPs must know what kind of applications AP-provided can be deployed to their resources. And prior to servicing to users, SP must know which applications have already been deployed and available. GridASP portal helps these complicated processes via Web-based interface. And it manages all deployment information in its own centralized database, because APs, RPs, and SPs are expected to have tight requirement for the state synchronization.

3.2. *Semi-automated Application Deployment*

As described in Figure 3, GridASP enables Semi-automated application deployment to any nodes of clusters which are owned by RPs and managed by

LSF, SGE, or PBS. Once APs prepared application packages including binary packages and deployment descriptions, they can be semi-automatically downloaded to clusters and unpackaged and deployed as GridASP-enabled applications. In the current GridASP implementation, application packages for deployment can include any type of binary packages such as RPM and tar+gzip, but application providers should manually generate a script how they deploy. We plan to employ several community efforts such as Rocks[6], so as to make it much easier to deploy applications. But we think there are no shortcuts for commercial scientific applications.

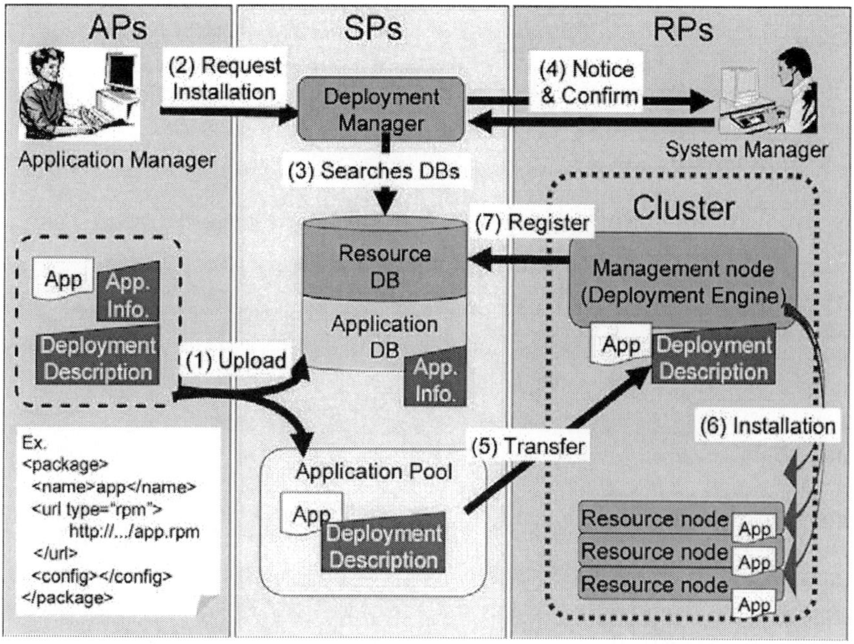

Figure 3 Centralized Application/Resource Management

3.3. *Anonymous IDs for RPs*

Though GridASP properly has enough security based on Grid Security Infrastructure (GSI) [7], it is not enough especially for enterprise users to conceal usage/computation information from other users, APs and RPs. Only SP should be able to access these kind of information for logging and accounting purpose. To conceal these information, GridASP maps real user IDs to anonymous IDs on the portal, prior to every job submissions and obfuscates "Who computes" information for APs and RPs (see Figure 4).

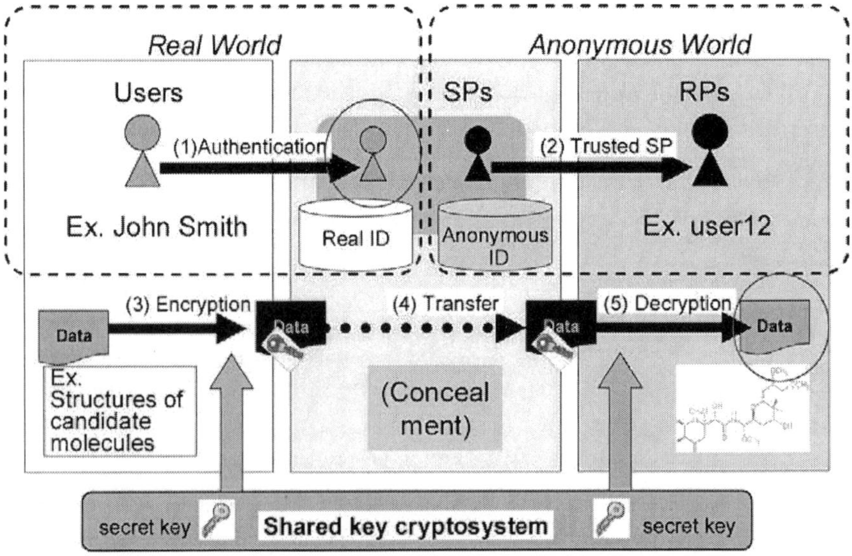

Figure 4 Security Architecture of GridASP Toolkit

3.4. *Data encryption for bypassing SPs*

Adding to the abovementioned anonymousness, GridASP enables data encryption for every data transfers between end users and RPs, which is based on shared key cryptosystem and completely prevents SPs from wiretapping described as in Figure 4. In this cryptosystem, Key Creation Center (KCC) which is isolated from any entities of GridASP generates one-time shared key for every data transfers between users and RPs, and the key is encrypted by using public keys for users and RPs and delivered to them. Then they can decrypt the encrypted key by their own private keys. After that, data transfers may perform under the shared key encryption. Therefore, SPs relay data transfer between users and RPs, but they cannot see the key and data in any way.

3.5. *Visualized Workflow-Job Editor*

GridASP provides a visualized workflow-job editor to users. Using this editor, users can generate the job workflow graphs and specify how they should be executed. And it also provides the feature to split workflow graphs into multiple sub-graphs. By using this feature, users can point out a bunch of jobs which are preferable to be executed on the same resource, and the resource broker will broker jobs to the appropriate computing resources based on these information. GridASP Workflow-Job Editor employs our own internal workflow-job representation rather than standardized representation such as Business Process Execution Language (BPEL) [8], just for easier implementation and smaller footprint.

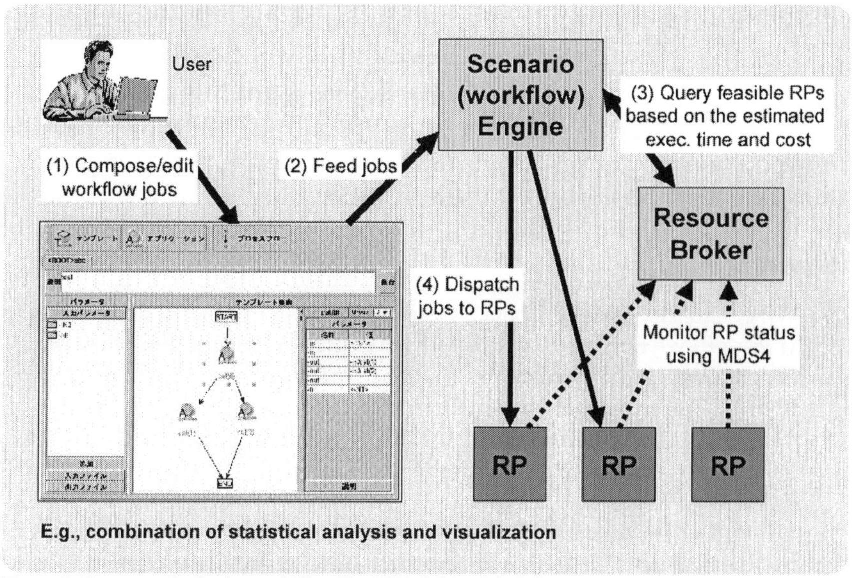

Figure 5 Resource Brokering and Visualized Workflow-Job Editor

3.6. *Resource Brokering based on user's preference*

GridASP Resource Broker monitors all RP status via MDS4, and appropriately brokers each job executions based on multiple policies such as cost-saving and time-saving. Users can choose the brokering policy at runtime via the portal Web interface.

4. Conclusion

The GridASP is a utility business framework for grid-enabled Application Service Providers (ASP) that supports technical enterprise applications such as Life sciences, Automotive, CAE, etc. In this paper, we reported the conceptual idea of GridASP and the detail of the framework now being developed. We have completed the first version of our GridASP framework in March 2005, and have published it as open source software under BSD-like license. Information on GridASP can be found on http://www.gridasp.org/. We are developing the second version which targets to the stability and availability for various cluster environments. The second version will be available at this early summer.

And, in order to verify the validity of our GridASP model, we are now conducting proof-of-concept experiments with various Japanese private companies including application vendors, data centers, and enterprise users. The result cannot be shown at this moment, but we will show the preliminary result in the presentation.

Acknowledgments

This paper and the development of GridASP framework are enforced as a part of Business Grid Computing Project led by METI, Japan.

References

1. Mary Thomas, Maytal Dahan, Kurt Mueller, Stephen Mock, Catherine Mills, Ray Regno, Application portals: practice and experience, *Concurrency and Computation: Practice and Experience*, 14(13-15). 1427-1443 (2002), http://gridport.net/.
2. Jason Novotny, Michael Russel, Oliver Wehrens, GridSphere: a portal framework for building collaborations, *Concurrency and Computation: Practice and Experience*, 16(5), 503-513 (2004), http://www.gridsphere.org/.
3. Apache Software Foundation, Jetspeed, http://portals.apache.org/jetspeed-1/.
4. Globus Alliance, Globus Toolkit, http://www-unix.globus.org/toolkit/.
5. Gregor von Laszewski, Ian Foster, Jarek Gawor, Peter Lane, A Java Commodity Grid Kit, *Concurrency and Computation: Practice and Experience*, 13(8-9), 643-662 (2001), http://www.globus.org/cog/java/.
6. Philip M. Papadopoulos, Mason J. Katz, and Greg Bruno, NPACI Rocks: Tools and Techniques for Easily Deploying Manageable Linux Clusters, *Concurrency and Computation: Practice and Experience (Special Issue: Cluster 2001)*.
7. Von Welch, Frank Siebenlist, Ian Foster, John Bresnahan, Karl Czajkowski, Jarek Gawor, Carl Kesselman, Sam Meder, Laura Pearlman, and Steven Tuecke, Security for Grid Services, *Twelfth International Symposium on High Performance Distributed Computing (HPDC-12)*, IEEE Press, June 2003.

8. Business Process Execution Language for Web Services version 1.1, IBM, BEA Systems, Microsoft, SAP AG, Siebel Systems, http://www-128.ibm.com/developerworks/library/specification/ws-bpel/.